Borders and Belonging

P38

Borders and Belonging

The Book of Ruth:
A Story for our Times

Pádraig Ó Tuama and
Glenn Jordan

CANTERBURY
PRESS
Norwich

Published in 2021 by Canterbury Press
Editorial office
3rd Floor, Invicta House,
108–114 Golden Lane,
London EC1Y OTG, UK
www.canterburypress.co.uk

Canterbury Press is an imprint of Hymns Ancient & Modern Ltd
(a registered charity)

HYMNS Ancient
&Modern

Hymns Ancient & Modern® is a registered trademark of
Hymns Ancient & Modern Ltd
13A Hellesdon Park Road, Norwich,
Norfolk NR6 5DR, UK

British Library Cataloguing in Publication data

A catalogue record for this book is available
from the British Library

978 1 786 22256 5

Scripture quotations are from New Revised Standard Version
Bible: Anglicized Edition, copyright © 1989, 1995 National
Council of the Churches of Christ in the United States of
America. Used by permission. All rights reserved worldwide.

The text of the Ruth Rabbah is available from www.sefaria.org/
Ruth_Rabbah?lang=bi in both English and Hebrew.

Typeset by Regent Typesetting

Glenn Jordan, 1964–2020

~ in ár gcroíthe go deo ~

Contents

Preface

As 2015 moved into 2016, I began to fear that British–Irish relations would regress rather than progress. Brexit was happening – and the rhetoric of Brexit echoed a wider rhetoric: blunt stories told poorly in order to push changes forward; changes that benefited some, devastated others, polarized many and built on stereotypes of the other that undid the possibility of a serious imagination of them.

What we needed was a story.

In the Brexit drama, the story of Britain and the story of Ireland is complicated. Where is Britain? Well, it's an island, but places outside that island – Northern Ireland in particular – also have stories of Britishness. Gibraltar too, and the Islas Malvinas.

Stories have the power to face us with ourselves. If a story is told well, it upsets some of our conveniences and challenges the previously unchallenged. Stories have unexpected twists and turns. Stories find heroes in strange corners. Stories reveal something about the behaviour of people previously considered to be above reproach. In stories we find our hearts drawn towards multiple characters, locating ourselves in the lives of this one and that one. Stories contain our projections and our prejudices, and – if we're lucky – we hear the story enough times that some of those projections and some of those prejudices are coaxed into a new imagination.

How does this happen? By telling the story. By listening to it. By hearing it anew. By exploring hitherto unexplored corners of it. By hearing how others read it. By a careful examination of the words. By holding many things at once: the story is true; the myth is truer than true; the events happened in this way; the story was told to challenge a people.

We are meaning-making, story-seeking people.

And so here – in the aftermath of 2016 and everything it brought, which is still unknown – is a story explored for our times: Ruth – a widowed border-crosser, a foreigner on land not her own, a character of virtue whose national belonging was viewed before her personhood.

I was busy, in 2016. I was leading Corrymeela, and poets are quick at some things but not at most. I needed help on the project. I knew that we needed to do something – find some story – to bring us together in the unfolding story of politics happening all around us. I phoned Glenn. As it happens, he was looking for some change. He said yes. I breathed a sigh of relief. It took ten minutes to explain the story to him. He got it. He started reading, he started writing.

Over the next few years, we – and when I say we, I mean mostly he – developed resources exploring Brexit, exploring belonging, exploring borders through the lens of the book of Ruth. We did not do this for the purposes of converting anyone to anything. We held meetings in Ireland, Scotland, Wales and England that brought together about 5,000 people in order to consider how the book of Ruth might speak to a quality and practice of belonging in the here and now. The 5,000 people voted differently. Some of them loved Britain. Some of them didn't. Some of them loved Ireland. Some of them didn't. At the beginning of a session we would often ask folks if they had a story in their family of someone who came from Ireland or went to Britain or married a Protestant when they shouldn't have or dated a Catholic. Stand up if you do; sit down if you don't. There was a rare person whose family history didn't include some kind of crossing, even within the boundaries of our small islands. We discovered new borders: Cornish people marrying outside Cornwall. Northumberland sadnesses remembered. Island people from places off the coast of Ireland or Scotland who viewed mainlanders with anxiety. Somebody spoke about the mainland once, and they were misunderstood. They were a Protestant from Belfast and the mainland – to them – was Britain. Someone else thought they were talking about France. What we call the places we turn to is different. We turn to different places. We start at different points of the story.

Five thousand people. Yes. Hungry. Sitting down in the grass. Is there food enough for us all? What scraps? What lessons? What baskets held the food? Who offered the small idea? Who made it grow into something that could feed a multitude? I don't know, really – nobody knows the author of the book of Ruth. What I can say is that the Irish government's Fund for Reconciliation was generous. I met with them to talk about the idea. They said, 'How much do you need?' I gave them a modest amount. They upped it. The Northern Ireland Community Relations Council also helped. Honestly, we didn't need much. Just some money for small salaries for writing. Mostly we met in homes and church halls, festival tents and corners of cathedrals. There were people in those meetings who loved religion and people who didn't. 'We're not here to make you holy', I'd often say. Glenn would usually mutter something about me not being holy myself. His mutterings were always gold.

What follows is an exploration of the magnificent book of Ruth, an exploration undertaken for the purposes of hope.

Can we find a story that might lead us to say things other than the things we are shouting at each other in the letters section of newspapers, comments sections of websites and social media, shouty parts of shouty programmes on radio and television? Can we be held in some kind of narrative creativity by a story whose origins we do not know?

We hope so.

We were two Irish men writing stories about a Moabite woman and her Jewish family. We recognize the audacity. We do not explore this story to own it; we explore it to honour it, knowing that we need to be changed, not it. Our explorations of how to read this story, and therefore how to read the question of today, overlaps, diverges, coalesces and contradicts. That's the point. We aren't presenting one way, we're telling stories of how we circled round this magnificent story during a time when we're sorely in need of the kind of stories that might help us tell better stories about each other.

Ruth is centre stage in this four-act drama. It is towards her that we turn. And it is towards her that the other characters in this story turn too. Or turn away, as some do. In the theatre of Ruth, a nation is asked to consider itself by its recognition of the power of kindness; not by its repetition of stereotype. The book of Ruth demands that people in the here and now speak to each other, rather than about each other. Surprising connections emerge; and the scandal that arises from such surprising connections is the stuff of politics and loyalty and division and cost. In all of it, Ruth stays steady. Who taught her such things? Herself, presumably.

Stories take strange turns and crises occur without warning: husbands die and famines arise and people are left without the plans they had so carefully prepared. In life too. Glenn died suddenly in June 2020, just nine weeks ago at time of writing. Reading his words in these chapters – we each wrote alternate chapters – is like eavesdropping into his political mind; his linguistic mind; his storytelling mind; his sharp intellect; his sharper wit; his whiskey glass raised making jokes about Corkmen, telling stories of the family he adored with his whole heart.

In the doorway to a book about a story, here's a little story.

I'd known Glenn since I was 11 and he was a dorm leader on a church camp. When I moved to Belfast 16 years later, I sought him out and we've remained friends ever since. I was working in religion and over-full of faith and fear. Faith kept me fearful, sometimes. Especially because I was gay and had told few people. On a drive back from a conference once, I told Glenn. I wasn't sure what he'd say. We continued in a lot of silence. When we parked, he turned to me and said, 'What you've said changes me.' I was mostly looking for acceptance and comfort. Glenn wasn't interested in that. He had heard something that had changed him. In the twinkling. He gave comfort, sure. But he acted differently. He manifested change in a way I could never have imagined. He lost friends because of it. He made me realize that I didn't need to be a pawn begging for the dregs of kindness. He took me seriously enough that I began to take myself seriously. He changed me in the way he changed. Glenn saw change as the demonstration of faithfulness, not the denial of it. I carry him in my heart.

It was impossible to know Glenn and not know his family. My Adrienne, he'd say; or my Philippa; or my CJ. His lovely rounded vowel sounds around that possessive *my*. Pride fit to bursting with joy and love fitted inside a small sound from his mouth. To be in his orbit was to know that his orbit was the orbit around his family. His brothers. His parents. His *my*. It is to them that this book owes its intellectual and theological imagination. To them belongs the thanks for being the cathedral of belonging from which Glenn's love sprung. And it is to them – and of course to Glenn – that this book is dedicated.

Pádraig Ó Tuama
Ireland, August 2020

I

Liturgical Setting of Ruth

GLENN JORDAN

Background to the book of Ruth

The Brexit referendum campaign in June 2016 and the subsequent triggering of Article 50 in March 2017 introduced
a new level of coarseness into political discourse on these
islands. It seems obvious now, as levels of vitriol have heightened and civilized conversation and debate have been stifled
on our streets, in the Houses of Parliament and even round
the family dinner table, that something deep and profound
has happened to our civic life. In Ireland, tensions have been
reignited in relation to the border between Northern Ireland
and the Republic of Ireland. A peace we once thought secure
has proved to be fragile and delicate, as peace often is. Meanwhile, in the United States we see the rising viability of old
supremacies: the rise of white nationalism, the separation of
children from their parents at the southern border, conserv-
ative Christians offering unwavering support to a president
who seems to revel in divisive language and questionable
behaviours.

The Christian Church hasn't exactly covered itself in glory
during this time of turmoil. In Ireland, the various institutions
emerged from the anguish and heartbreak of the Troubles to
find congregations and parishes traumatized and angry, and

a leadership ill-equipped to deal with the task of taking our society towards reconciliation. We were better pastors to our 'own' than we were prophets to our community. Clergy and lay leaders in congregations and parishes from the north and south of Ireland professed to us their caution about addressing the issue of the referendum because of its divisiveness.

In Britain, the Church of England found that parishioners were radically at odds with their clergy, particularly the House of Bishops. Indeed, membership of the Church of England, it turns out, is a reliable indicator of a vote to leave the EU. Exit polling on the day of the referendum showed that 66 per cent of voters identifying as Church of England voted to leave the EU, which is higher than England as a whole (53 per cent). In contrast, only one Anglican bishop is on record as having supported Leave. With such a contrast between laity and leadership it is no surprise that Anglican comment on the Brexit divisions has been so convoluted. In the United States, however, things are very different in some ways, and depressingly familiar in others. It has been frequently noted that 81 per cent of self-identified white evangelical voters cast a ballot for Donald Trump in the 2016 presidential election, and that number has barely shifted in the years since, despite all that has happened. No matter what the constitution may say about the separation of church and state in the United States, they seem now, to an outsider, to be inextricably linked. The lines of identity have been drawn so clearly and indelibly that civil conversation across the borders of belonging seems to be incredibly difficult, if not impossible.

At first glance the book of Ruth wasn't the obvious place to go to for wisdom in navigating this fraught territory. Indeed, the contrast between this biblical narrative of kindness and compassion couldn't be starker when compared to the bear pit of politics and civic discourse in recent years on the issue of the EU. But maybe that is exactly why Ruth is important for us today when kindness and compassion seem to be in such short supply. This apparently simple book situates itself at the very places where the tectonic plates of conflicted communities threaten to crack and split apart whole nations and societies. Perhaps it offers us a way towards the healing of our fractures and the building of new and healthy relationships in the aftermath of trauma. This narrative enters into the conversation, or the silence, between us, not to exacerbate our divisions but as a spotlight and a balm, pointing to a better way of handling our differences.

However, as a first step, we have a stereotype to overcome. We are perhaps most familiar with the words of this book as it is used in some wedding ceremonies. Ruth's transcendent language of love and loyalty in 1.16–17 is often spoken from one partner to the other as part of the liturgy. The book is thus often perceived as a romantic story of the young, beautiful woman fallen on hard times who meets a good man; they fall in love, get married and have a child. There is a faint hint of some questionable behaviour on the way through but this is artfully covered, though only barely.

As we engage deeper with the story and with the lives of the characters, other profound things begin to reveal themselves: the mystery of relationships between women; the trauma of surviving one's children; the pain of childlessness; the challenge of marriage and patriarchy. And as we think about contemporary politics, the story features a number of border-crossings: Elimelech and his wife Naomi and their two sons leave Bethlehem because of famine and move across a border to the country of their traditional enemy, Moab. There they settle and the boys find wives, but tragedy is never far from their door. Pretty soon Elimelech dies, followed by both of his sons, and we are left with three widows.

In her grief Naomi decides to return home and does so in the company of one of her daughters-in-law, Ruth. Now Ruth, in her turn, crosses a border and becomes a stranger in a land with a long history of antagonism towards the land of her birth. Not only is she an ethnic stranger, she is also a woman in a man's world, a foreigner in a country that doesn't like her sort, childless in a society that required sons, a widow in a family-based culture and poor in a community that lacked a comprehensive safety net. She is therefore uniquely vulnerable.

The book challenges us on welcoming the stranger; on re-drawing our stereotypes through encounter with those who are 'other'; on finding gaps where compassion can thrive in the midst of technical debates about law and tradition; on carrying losses that cannot be grieved. It presents us with questions of how to protect the rights of vulnerable minorities, particularly those who are politically and socially marginal, and it also challenges the careful reader as to the responsibility of those who are financially and socially secure towards the poor. This short narrative features those who are forced to migrate to another country because of poverty or famine and therefore encourages communities to face the question of what constitutes national identity and belonging.

It may therefore be *the* book in the Hebrew Bible that is uniquely suited to our time and place. It may not deliver answers directly fitted to the issues of our day, but it may help us form better questions as we explore what it is to be communities of faith now. As such Ruth may also empower us to take an effective place in the public square where decisions are being made that affect the lives of millions, and also help us amplify those voices silenced in the clamour of political, economic and social debates.

Liturgical setting in Judaism

Since the book of Ruth is part of the Hebrew Bible it is worth considering how it is used within Jewish tradition. Ruth is part of what is known as the *Megilloth*, or the Five Small Scrolls, comprising the books of Ruth, Esther, Ecclesiastes, Song of Songs and Lamentations. Each of these is associated exclusively with one of Judaism's five main annual festivals and is read in its entirety alongside a specially chosen text from the Torah, or the books of Moses.

The book of Ruth is associated with the festival of Shavuot, or what Christians know as the Feast of Pentecost, and the assigned portion of Torah is Exodus 19 and 20, which tells the story of the giving of the Law to Moses on Mount Sinai. This liturgical setting is fascinating. The Exodus reading is epic and magnificent, full of fiery images of smoky mountains and trembling earth. All the senses are engaged by thunder and lightning and deafening trumpet blasts. Consider this passage:

On the morning of the third day there was thunder and lightning, as well as a thick cloud on the mountain, and a blast of a trumpet so loud that all the people who were in the camp trembled. Moses brought the people out of the camp to meet God. They took their stand at the foot of the mountain. Now Mount Sinai was wrapped in smoke, because the LORD had descended upon it in fire; the smoke went up like the smoke of a kiln, while the whole mountain shook violently. As the blast of the trumpet grew louder and louder, Moses would speak and God would answer him in thunder ... Then the LORD said to Moses, 'Go down and warn the people not to break through to the Lord to look; otherwise many of them will perish.' (Ex. 19.16–19, 21)

These are the particulars surrounding the giving of the Ten Commandments, and they are terrifying. So terrifying and dangerous, in fact, that the people are instructed to build some kind of a fence around the base of the mountain to prevent any living being from approaching and touching it. The presence of God on the mountain makes the whole thing holy and God's holiness deals death to people. The sheer spectacle of what happens when God draws near drains the people of any courage whatsoever; they stress to Moses that they only want to hear God's voice, and so they remain at a distance (Ex. 20.18–19, 21).

There is a small but extraordinary detail in the middle of this tumultuous story that is worth noting. The account tells us that a lone human voice pierces all the din and is heard and finds a divine voice responding (Ex. 19.19).

It is perhaps this small detail that provides a clue as to why this story accompanies the book of Ruth at the feast of Shavuot. On the surface there is no obvious thematic connection to tie these stories together. One is a drama on a cinematic scale, the other a quiet narrative of human endurance, an intimate story of survival in the face of the overwhelmingly terrible ordinary. Ruth is a much more relatable tale that narrates hunger, bereavement, isolation and hard work in the struggle to survive as a migrant. There are also simple human kindnesses that are ultimately transformational in that they result in the securing of a place for displaced people. These generous acts also result in the transformation of the lives of those who extended the kindnesses. Ruth finds belonging and kinship as a result of her loyalty to Naomi; Boaz, the wealthy landowner who opens first his fields and then his home life to a stranger, finds a wife, then a child and a permanent foothold in the history of his people; and Naomi finds a place, a home and a secure future that transforms an earlier bitterness.

The community these people are a part of is also transformed. The unfolding of the story sees the community managing to overcome its antipathy and suspicion towards the stranger from Moab. In doing so it reaches a new understanding of itself, crafts a new system of laws that pays attention to the plight of the vulnerable, and welcomes someone into the web of kinship who would otherwise be excluded.

There is nothing small about human survival in the face of grave danger or peril, nor anything trifling about a community opening its doors and its heart to the stranger. Nevertheless, when placed alongside the Torah portion, the human scale of these challenges to the human spirit can be overshadowed by the drama of Sinai's ground-shaking events. This is perhaps a part of the reason why Jewish liturgists connected these two stories together for Pentecost.

Keeping perspective in world-changing events

The festival liturgy connects the struggles of human individuals with the great mountain-shaking events of Sinai. It thus preserves the significance of the common experience of a human person in the face of great world-making events and dares us to find ways to make personal what could otherwise be overwhelming. The festival of Shavuot celebrates the giving of the Law; therefore to have that giving accompanied by the transformative generous lives of ordinary individuals is surely of some significance.

It is challenging to pick out a face in the crowd huddled in terror around the base of Mount Sinai. The scene is too overwhelming; the senses are overcome by noise and light and we are distracted by our terror. But we know from the circumstances of our own lives that among this mass of people there were new parents trying to get their baby to sleep; there were those noticing worrying changes in their ageing bodies; some were still traumatized by all the ugliness and death they had seen during the horror of slavery. Everyone in that crowd, pressed together in terror at a distance from Mount Sinai, was there in the enormity of their own humanity. It is easy to forget this in the din of spectacle. And in the end what they looked for was not the booming voice of God like some terrifying Wizard of Oz, but the real human voice of the one who got to step behind the curtain. So they ask for Moses to mediate the words of God to them.

When we read this account in Exodus, important though it undoubtedly is, it is easy for us to miss the story's humanity. Maybe this is why we are invited to read it alongside the human-scale story of Ruth. It reminds us to keep our eyes and ears alert for the small dramas that constitute the lives of most and to avoid being distracted by the hoopla of the dancing mountain.

In recent years we have lived through an extraordinary display of politics, economics and international relationships. A future generation of history or politics students will look back with rigour and marvel at how we did what we did. We live in ground-shaking times, whether it is the incredible Brexit drama in Westminster in the autumn of 2019, or the nervousness around the British border in Ireland during that same period. Similarly, we could look to the suffering at the southern border of the United States or the political intrigue between the legislative and executive branches of government there; the street protests in Hong Kong; the kinetic warfare in Libya, Syria, Yemen or Afghanistan; or cyber warfare between West and East. It is tempting to be seduced into imagining that this is all of life; that what great people do on the global stage is of supreme importance.

The book of Ruth reminds us to look to the margins and to ask about who is being affected by these global eruptions. The bright and shiny baubles of Brexit, for instance, are overwhelmingly powerful, but they can also distract us from what is going on behind the loud exterior. Ruth reminds us that there will always be those driven back by the noise, pinned down by the tumult, who will be seeking mediating voices to speak to them words of comfort and inclusion and assure them they have not been forgotten.

The shaping worth of liturgy

This is why good liturgy, entered into over the span of a life, is so important. When texts, prayers and responses embed themselves deep within us we are unconsciously shaped and formed by those performances and rituals. Every human life has these sacred ways. They can be as simple and honest as doing the laundry or making tea, or as complex as communion or baptism. There are equally rituals and habits of performance that dehumanize both the object and the subject of those acts. These are countless sacramental acts that go to make a life. The familiarity of sacred ways and habits that are repeated time and again are more than mere experiences to be accumulated, they are a way of living. Thus, the regular coupling of the book of Ruth, with its familiar scale of narrative, and the monumental, even bombastic adventures at Mount Sinai train the ears of the participants for the thin voices of those who struggle to find their footing in troubled times.

Yet in such divisive times it is a real challenge to find the words and actions that embody our conflicts in healthy ways by naming them, by holding them up to public scrutiny and through corporate engagement to find ways of healing them. It is a challenge because in the practice of our faith we know that congregations and parishes, families and friendships have fractured under the pressure of our differences. Faith leaders sometimes think that worship should be the very place where people can find respite from the things that divide us in the rest of life. But good liturgy, which is the kind of liturgy that emerges from the reality of human lives, does not shirk from standing right in the middle of the noise and tumult of our times and mediating the divine to us.

We must dare to find creative and apparently disruptive couplings of words and actions that both reflect back to us the reality of the divisions we face by naming what it is that divides us but also alert us to what we have missed because of the distractions of our conflicts.

Ruth as a hermeneutical lens

There is one final consideration on the issue of this strange and intriguing partnership between the Exodus text and the book of Ruth. A key word in Ruth is the Hebrew *chesed*, which is often translated as 'lovingkindness'. This word is often understood in terms of generous and kind acts that an individual chooses to do in favour of another. And while such an act may be towards someone we know or are related to in some way, by blood or ethnicity for instance, they are most particularly kind acts that are done despite obvious differences and which we are not obligated to perform. In Jewish tradition, *chesed* is a vital contribution to *tikkun olam*, the repairing of the world.

Law by itself cannot do this, even though Law – Torah in Hebrew – is the beloved ground on which this work of repair can happen. Law can compel acts of generosity but it cannot supply the magnanimity that draws generous actions from us in places where the Law doesn't extend. When, year after year at Shavuot, Jewish worshippers hear this Torah portion read alongside the book of Ruth, it establishes an ongoing dialogue between Law and lovingkindness. It may very well be that this humble story of simple human kindness is the proper lens through which the Law of Moses should be read.

If true, this presents us with a radical challenge. It suggests that the story of Ruth is the proper hermeneutic for interpreting the purpose of the Law and should therefore alert us to the fact that kindness and love for the other, rather than ritual purity, is the proper intent of the Law. Year after year at Pentecost, Jews are reminded not to be seduced by the notion that God can be satisfied by ticking off fulfilment of the Law. Judaism's liturgy highlights that it is possible to keep the Law perfectly and yet still be devoid of kindness. The Law – made present through liturgy – declares that it cannot fully heal the world, only kindness and generosity can do that. Such public liturgical reminders are needed in all community-making and nation-making structures.

For many people, Brexit is a distant thing that, while they know it will affect their lives, ultimately they are powerless to do anything about. The temptation with this feeling of impotence is to disengage and to try and ensure that 'I and my family' can navigate these choppy waters while leaving others to fend for themselves. At a national level, there will be a temptation to revert to legal definitions and the creation of impersonal international agreements that in their application find limited space or patience for the plight of ordinary lives. In addition, sheer complexity and divisiveness, coupled with the awful weariness created by Brexit, may mean that we will resist the careful and sustained analysis required to understand why Europe has been the cause of so much hostility for some in Britain. In all sorts of ways, therefore, Brexit mitigates against acts of kindness and generosity.

Thus, we must resist the urge to separate the pain of Brexit from the practice of faith. The book of Ruth invites us to something much more challenging, complex and ultimately healing, for us and for the world. It invites us to examine the importance and the limitations of law but more importantly to consider the enduring and transformative impact of kindness and generosity, not just for politics and international relationships but for all our encounters in the world.

The First Act of the Book of Ruth

PÁDRAIG Ó TUAMA

No Ammonite or Moabite shall be admitted to the assembly of the Lord. Even to the tenth generation, none of their descendants shall be admitted to the assembly of the Lord. (Deut. 23.3)

Ask anyone about the book of Ruth and – if they know it – they'll say something about Ruth and Naomi and Where-You-Go-I-Will-Go and maybe something about Moab and something about threshing floors. It is a fast-paced theatrical biblical book that – while it mentions a God, and is certainly set on the stage of Judaism – does not have any divine interventions. As a piece of drama this story unfolds brilliantly, in four chapters, or – to speak theatrically – four acts. Each act has its own setting; each act flows from itself into the next.

An act within theatre comes from the Latin word *āctus*, meaning a *doing*, *a thing done* or *something set in motion*. Like all good stories, the book of Ruth has dramatic wheels in motion from the very moment the story opens: 'In the days when the judges ruled, there was a famine in the land.'

This functions as a timestamp, except a timestamp for a time apart from the one in which it is written. We are about to hear a story about a particular time and particular people, but first of all the setting is given. Judges had a clear mandate:

to highlight injustice, to highlight hypocrisy, to call the people back to the God they followed. The judges were less legislative arbiters and more leaders. They were not monarchs, nor were they elected, nor were they hereditary. The offspring of one judge were not assumed to be the judges of the newer generation. So the book establishes itself as being written in a time of a particular style of leadership.

'Judge' is both a noun and a verb. A more accurate translation of the first verse of this story might be, 'And it was in the days when the judges judged'. Listen to that: judges judged: a little sonic mirror holding the word 'judge' up to itself. The book of Ruth is a text about leadership and law and those who claim to uphold them, as well as those who claim to represent them. Given that, it is notable that in the opening verses, three males are disposed of: Naomi's husband and two sons all die at the beginning of this story, which gallops through famine and displacement, marriage and bereavement. Who is being judged here? What are they being judged for? For not showing kindness? All these questions are opened in this dramatic narrative.

Not only are we placed in the time of judges, we are also placed in a time of famine. The Hebrew word for 'famine' – *rā'āb* – can also be used for 'hunger'. Hebrew isn't unique in this; Irish does the same. We call the famine of the 1840s *an Gorta Mór* – the Great Hunger. Famine is a familiar story in the Hebrew Bible, from Abram to Joseph and David:

> Now there was a famine in the land. So Abram went down to Egypt to reside there as an alien. (Gen. 12.10)

> ... and the seven years of famine began to come, just as Joseph had said. (Gen. 41.54)

Now there was a famine in the days of David for three years, year after year. (2 Sam. 21.1)

Famine is associated with multiple powers in the Hebrew Bible. Often it is narrated with the experience of displacement and also, obviously, death. However, in biblical literature, famine is sometimes wielded as a metaphor, a power in the hand of God, who holds back crops so that people can learn their mistakes, wrongdoings or betrayals. This mythic quality of storytelling, often used in national narratives, sees the events of a particular time as a window through which the state of a people can be viewed. The writer of the book of Ruth – and we do not know her name – saw Ruth's story as such a window. Open the window of leadership, open the window of famine, open the window of a displaced woman from a hated country – with these windows open, the story of the book flows in.

So it is leadership and hunger – and, by association, a hunger for leadership – that the book of Ruth uses to establish the opening imagination for this extraordinary story. It is a book about Law and those who lead the people in lawmaking, lawbreaking and law reshaping.

Any story is an interaction between setting, plot and character:

A person goes on a journey.
   From where to where?
      What's going to happen?
      Who is this person?

A stranger comes to town.
   Where did they come from?
      Why?
      Who are they?

In this context, a few journeys happen. Naomi leaves Bethlehem with her husband and sons; they go to Moab, the boys marry local women; all the men die; the three women – two locals and a foreigner – are left with each other; the foreigner decides to return home and tells the local women to return to their mothers; one does, the other doesn't; two women arrive back in Bethlehem; they aren't saying much to each other.

The plot of the book of Ruth is a subtle mix of things that cannot be controlled and things that can. Naomi is married to a man named Elimelech. Not much is said about him, which in itself says a lot. The commentaries of the Midrash – particularly the Ruth Rabbah – give us some background. 'Midrash' is another term that is both noun and verb. As a noun it refers to writings and interpretations on the Hebrew Bible, writings that function like a psychoanalysis of the text; as verb it refers to the capacity to ask good questions of the text, knowing that the text is robust enough for any question that can be asked of it. Written Midrash gathers questions that sages and rabbis have asked throughout centuries and poses them alongside each other, not for the sake of ending an argument but for enlivening one. It's hard to tell, sometimes, where the midrashic narratives that enliven the text come from. Is it from the deep history of the words used, or from centuries of speculation about the omission of a certain word? Is the information part of an oral tradition that had *always* been known, or is it what one person thought should be the case in order for the story to make sense? Whatever the origin, the Midrash asks interesting questions, like this one: why was Elimelech punished?

The Midrash considers this question by noting that while Elimelech's name meant 'To me will come kingship', he didn't act much like a king. When famine came, he did nothing to support the local town. His maid went to the market with an empty basket, and when people saw this they despaired, because if her basket was empty, then they had no hope. Elimelech realized that everyone would come asking him for provisions and he didn't want this. So he fled (Ruth Rabbah, chapter 1).

There is withdrawal elsewhere in this first chapter too. Naomi – after her husband and sons have died – is overwhelmed. She's clear on one thing: she does not want her daughters-in-law with her. She seeks to withdraw from their lives and the country she's come to call home. She sends Ruth and Orpah home to their mothers; Orpah goes and disappears from the narrative. Naomi, however, has met her match in Ruth, who refuses, and seems to counteract every point that Naomi makes.

In the course of our project on Brexit and the book of Ruth, we encountered a lot of discussion about Ruth's beautiful lines, 'Where you go, I will go ...'. Some saw Ruth's assertion as a demonstration of love for her mother-in-law. Others asked whether there could have been an erotic link between the women (and indeed, there's linguistic reason: Ruth *clings* to her mother-in-law, the same word used to describe how a man will *cling* to his wife; see Genesis 2.24); still others wondered if Ruth had become a convert to the Jewish faith that she saw in her beloved Naomi. This final consideration is also the subject of much speculation from the rabbis. In the Midrash, it's noted that Naomi ordered Ruth and Orpah to turn back three times (vv. 8, 11 and 12), much as any potential convert to Judaism is refused three times in order to test their resolve. If they try again after that, then the discussions can start (Ruth Rabbah, chapter 2). In everyday conversations in church halls in Belfast or Dublin or Glasgow, participants venture into the realm of ancient midrashic texts without knowing. Why did Ruth go and Orpah not? Was Naomi's grief for her dead sons, or her return, or her departure? What was it like to return home? Would Naomi have left Moab for Israel if she hadn't been so bereaved? Why did she want to go alone? Did she want to die along the way? Why was Ruth so determined to go with her? Did she know the danger she was facing? Did they talk much along the way? Was Ruth's presence a comfort to her mother-in-law, or did Naomi resent having to care for this Moabite from Moab who was now a widowed border-crosser. How old was Naomi? How old was Ruth?

None of these questions are answerable, which is their glory. And the text is so determined to rest in its four powerful acts that it omits much detail from the lives of people who already – even after one simple chapter – have become impressed on the reader's mind. In so doing, the text provides a container for the readers, while also allowing for many small openings through which the imagination can travel. In times of distress about global borders – borders in and around Europe, imperial borders, armed borders, disputed borders – there is much to talk about. But when borders, and their narratives, are disputed, the story about those borders is also disputed. Who put them there? Are they 'natural'? Who defines what a natural border is? Whether it's stories of border-straddling farms on the British border drawn across Ireland, or stories of border-crossing people swimming across the Rio Grande, there is need for a simple story to trouble the simple stories we sometimes tell about borders. The book of Ruth creates such a narrative. Fiction or fact – we'll get to that later – it is comprehensive and sufficient.

Where was Moab anyway? It was a neighbouring territory and – as will be discussed in the next chapter – was a territory associated with animosity. Over and over, Ruth is named as Ruth the Moabite:

So Naomi returned together with Ruth the Moabite, her daughter-in-law, who came back with her from the country of Moab. (1.22)

And Ruth the Moabite said to Naomi ... (2.2)

Then Ruth the Moabite said ... (2.21)

Then Boaz said, 'The day you acquire the field from the hand of Naomi, you are also acquiring Ruth the Moabite ...' (4.5)

'I have also acquired Ruth the Moabite ...' (4.10)

The one instance where the word 'Moabite' is used in the text without formally naming Ruth seems self-conscious in this lack of clarity. So to clear up any confusion, she is referred to as the Moabite from Moab: 'She is the Moabite who came back with Naomi from the country of Moab' (2.6).

What is this frenzy of naming? Moabites had a bad reputation among Israelites – and, to be clear, vice versa. Neither territory liked the other, and stories were told in Israel that caricatured the women of Moab as sex-crazed people. Along these lines, one strange little throwaway text in the Midrash on Ruth suggests that 'everyone who saw her orgasmed' (attributed to Rabbi Yochanan, Ruth Rabbah, chapter 4). Why would this be? The crudity of the statement projects dripping sexuality on to Ruth, but even a simple exploration of this sentence should begin to query the 'everyone' rather than the 'her'.

Everyone? Really? Is that possible? Who is saying this? What is it like to be a person whose presence in a place arouses all kinds of reactions in your onlookers? Is the implication that the narrator and the onlookers are male? Had the story of the Moabite women so impressed centuries of men from Bethlehem that they couldn't see her without thinking of sex? Whose fault was that? Not Ruth's, certainly. To be the walking witness of an identity that has been the cruel focus of others' eroticized projections is a path lined with the bombs of other people's unexplored hostility. Because – as Tamar discovers elsewhere in the Hebrew narrative – the power of desire is matched only by the destruction that desire denies: 'Then Amnon was seized with a very great loathing for her; indeed his loathing was even greater than the lust he had felt for her' (2 Sam. 13.15).

Who is this woman, the object of so many people's gaze? Ruth is gazed upon by Naomi, who does not seem to want her company. She is gazed upon also, at the end of the first act of the story, by the inhabitants of the city, who are all out when she and Naomi arrive in Bethlehem after their trek from Moab. The Midrash explains that all the people of Bethlehem were out to mark the funeral of Boaz's wife. The people function almost like a Greek chorus – of comedy and tragedy and everything in between – commenting and gossiping about the return of the wife of the man who fled when he should have stayed.

Oh, how we love a drama. And how much hostility lurks behind the gossipy gaze.

To return home is no return at all. I wonder regularly what Naomi meant to do if she had been allowed to travel back alone. She was empty already, and she's even changed her name – from Naomi, meaning 'sweet', to Mara, meaning 'bitter' – so I usually assume she wished to walk into her own ending, in the in-between borders between the place she came from and the place she went to.

Anyway, back to orgasms: whether Ruth caused spontaneous

eruptions in all the bodies, some of the bodies or none of the bodies, she was a Moabite body herself – as the text refuses to forget – and simply for that, there was a law about her:

> No Ammonite or Moabite shall be admitted to the assembly of the LORD. Even to the tenth generation, none of their descendants shall be admitted to the assembly of the LORD, because they did not meet you with food and water on your journey out of Egypt, and because they hired against you Balaam son of Beor, from Pethor of Mesopotamia, to curse you. (Deut. 23.3–4)

Because of what *your* people did to *our* people – back in the time when we've forgotten who started what – we hold this against you today. It is a repeated story: because of what x did to y; because z started it; because we cannot forget q. It is repeated because it's powerful, and Ruth is walking into a time-warp, where what was done in the mythologized past is remembered in the real present, and what is remembered is re-membered, so she, in the membership of her own body, is the blank canvas upon which hate-filled histories hang. It would be comic – or tragic – if it were not so common, so powerful and so true. We do this to each other all the time, and for what seems like good reason. Peoples have treated other peoples like vermin (if we tortured vermin to death in slow, painful, considered ways), and often the perpetrators of this hatred deny this hatred happened, and so the living descendants are bearing witness to truth and life by remembering themselves.

In one congregation in Dublin we asked people: 'What do your people hold against people from other jurisdictions around Ireland and Britain?' There were folks with links to both Irish jurisdictions there, as well as Welsh, Scottish and

English. There was even a Cornish person in the mix. We asked the question. Someone said, 'I wouldn't like to repeat such things in a church.' We laughed, but we said, 'Try.' Try because it's better to name the things we hold against each other for all the truthing, birthing, dying, changing energies that are needed. What is not remembered is repeated, Freud said, so we remembered hatreds and pains. And there were many. Our language was taken. My son was murdered. Our place was terrorized. Our reputation was ridiculed. You discover new things when you name your hatreds of peoples to people who are part of those peoples.

Thus far, the book of Ruth is presenting the relationships of Israelite and Moabite territories through the characters of Ruth and Naomi. If the title and unfolding of the book were unknown, one might wonder who is going to take the stage in the subsequent chapters. But as the title implies, it is Ruth – the Moabite from Moab – whose body and story and actions are central. In the dramatic storytelling that unfolds, it is easy to forget that this story is telling more than the story of individual border-crossing women. In a time of judging judges, someone has chosen to write a story where a woman's courage is the thing that returns a people to themselves.

The book is implying that Ruth might be in the image of a true judge, a true leader. Having had judges from across the twelve tribes, now a writer proposes that a displaced foreign widowed woman who crossed a border with her bereft mother-in-law is a judge; and she rules not by enunciations but by embodying *chesed*. It is she who – in her subsequent bravery, survival and encounters – brings about a change in the people who will eventually count her as one of their own. She, who is not one of them, turned to join Naomi as she returned home, and Ruth, in her turn, turns a people to the best of themselves.

3

Addressing Stereotypes

GLENN JORDAN

A relief from violence

Though set in the time of the judges, the story of Ruth is an oasis of calm in the hostility of the period. The book of Judges is set in a time of lawlessness and violence; indeed, the opening verse sets the tone when the people ask the Lord to identify the ones who would lead their fight against the Canaanites (Judg. 1.1). By the end of verse 4 in chapter 1, 10,000 men have been killed and the king of the Canaanites has had his thumbs and big toes removed (v. 6). Presumably this was to prevent him from wielding a sword or running into battle any time in the future, rendering the warrior dependent on others as an invalid. It's an early example of the principle of an eye for an eye, recognized as a punishment from God for the prior cruelty of Adoni-bezek, the king in question, who had inflicted the same punishment on rulers he had earlier defeated (1.7).

There is no let-up in the brutality of Judges; indeed, it gets worse as the book progresses. It lays the blame squarely on the generation of people who followed Joshua and those who had personally experienced the early conquest of the land, who are described as a people who neither knew the Lord nor what he had done for Israel (2.10). What follows is a repeated cycle of apostasy, followed by oppression, followed by the rise of a successful military leader who frees them from their enemies, followed by a period of peace, followed by apostasy again. And again. And again. The stories are fierce, frequently brutish and inhuman; Ehud buries a knife in the fat of a king's belly and walks calmly away (3.21–23); Jael drives a tent-peg through the temple of Sisera and pins him to the ground with it (4.21); Gideon tortures 77 men of Succoth by tearing their flesh with thorns and briers (8.16); Jephthah rashly makes a vow to the Lord in order to secure victory, and ends up sacrificing his only child, his young daughter (11.30–39); an unnamed Levite dismembers his unnamed concubine after she had been raped and raises and army to avenge her by sending her body parts all around the country (19.29–30). By the end of this relentless tale of horror and conflict the tribes have turned in on themselves and the book ends with the weary description that this was a time when 'all the people did what was right in their own eyes' (21.25).

The book of Ruth appears as a brief interlude between tales of war and empire building, offering us respite in a story of love and loyalty. It also offers more than that.

Here we should take a pause to note the differences in canonical order between the Jewish Bible and the Christian Bible. In the Jewish Bible, known as the *Tanakh*, the book of Ruth is part of the *Ketuvim* or Writings, accompanying the other four scrolls of the *Megilloth*, namely Song of Songs, Lamentations, Ecclesiastes and Esther. These five books, which are scattered in the Christian Bible, are given a prominence in the *Tanakh* because of their liturgical importance for the Jewish holidays. But in the Christian Bible the book of Ruth is tucked in between the book of Judges and 1 Samuel, probably because it is set there chronologically and also because it introduces David, the major character of I and II Samuel.

For Christian readers, therefore, what we encounter in the story of Ruth is not a continuation of the savagery of Judges but a book standing in gentle contrast to offer us relief from its ferocity. But by its end it goes further and Ruth offers us an alternative path to the aggression and toxic masculinity of the prior book. That the story is one that spotlights for us the place of a foreigner among the people of Israel should also halt us in our tracks, particularly after all the stories of aggression against foreigners as enemies.

Not much has changed

In truth, though, the reader is not completely done with stories of pain and dread. The opening line of the book of Ruth sets us within a context of violence ('In the days when the judges ruled') and of famine ('there was a famine in the land', Ruth 1.1). The cyclical violence of the time period and the impact of famine means life is precarious and unpredictable. There is an incredible drama behind the matter-of-fact statement that a man from Bethlehem, together with his wife and two sons, went to live for a time in the country of Moab (1.1). For instance, how long did it take and how hungry did they have to be before they took the decision to become refugees? It appears that we can't turn the page quite so easily on the trauma of what has gone before. Ongoing cycles of conflict and war affect not just human lives but the health of the very land on which we live and depend.

Right from the opening lines of this story we are being set up to expect something strange and unusual. There is a famine in Bethlehem, which in Hebrew means 'House of Bread'. If even the house of bread can experience a famine then what, if anything, can be relied on? This is a truth behind any war or famine which causes mass movement of populations. All this detail is given to us before the people concerned are named. It is perhaps a hint that this particular family are only representative of a whole community impacted by the food shortages. This family may be named but they do not represent in themselves the full measure of distress. And so in just the opening two verses we are introduced to a population who have crossed a river and a border to live in the land of Moab because of a famine. Actually, living in Moab is mentioned twice in the first two verses of the book.

Very quickly we find that the displacement across national borders is but one of the problems this family faces. Following the flight to Moab, Elimelech dies. Was it the exertion of the journey? The impact of war? The stress of the decision? The loss of hope? Who knows. Once again the writer states it in a matter-of-fact way and we are given no details; perhaps we are being left to imagine it for ourselves. The reader is then told that the two boys marry two Moabite women, who are named as Orpah and Ruth. This may seem like a tiny bright spot in the gloom of the story so far, but not really. To the original hearers of this story, while marriage in more favourable circumstances might be a joyful thing, marriage in the foreign land to which you have fled because of famine at home, and to Moabite women, is scandalous. And at the third mention of Moab in four verses we are forced to take note.

Israel has a history with Moab and it's not a pretty one. The artist behind this tale chooses Moab for very deliberate reasons. The text reminds us many times that Ruth is a woman from Moab (1.4, 22; 2.2, 6, 10, 21; 4.5, 10). There is also a certain amount of implied scandal in the fact that

Elimelech has fled with his family to escape the famine. Elimelech's name can mean 'God is my King' or alternatively, 'May kingship come my way', suggesting he is a man of substance, and we could perhaps assume that some resources were required simply to make the journey. In some streams of Jewish tradition, however, his reputation is cast in shadow because he did not stay to share what he had with those who were in need in his hometown. That he flees to Moab is of immense significance because in Hebrew folklore Moab was stereotyped as a place lacking in hospitality, and with some justification.

There is a memory preserved in the words of the Torah from another time of hunger and distress. In Numbers 22, the Israelites, recently freed from Egypt, are travelling through the wilderness on the way to the land of promise and they camp in the land of Moab. There is a reference in Deuteronomy 23.4 to a request made by the people to the Moabites for bread and water. The king of the Moabites, Balak, terrified by the number of people he would be required to supply and aware of their supposed reputation for 'licking up everything around them' (Num. 22.4), refuses their request for aid and shelter. Balak even hires a man to pronounce curses on them as he expels them from his land.

For contemporary readers of the book of Ruth this subtext may lie deeply hidden, but for those to whom the story was first told it would be obvious and cogent. The prejudgement of the original hearers is that in a time of hunger no sensible person in Judah looks to their neighbour Moab for help, for memory of famine, and particularly memory of treatment at the hands of a neighbouring nation who could help but didn't, is not easily forgotten, indeed can last for centuries. To make the connection to today, to a great extent, relationships between Britain and Ireland, and particularly between

England and Ireland, are still impacted by what happened during the Irish potato famine of 1845–9.

In 1845 the potato crop failed, falling victim to a blight that had made its way across Europe in the preceding years. It was the first year of what has become known as the Great Famine, or *an Gorta Mór*, the great hunger. By 1849 a million people had died, a million had emigrated and almost two million refugees roamed the land in search of food. These years began a century of emigration and have entered the folk memory of Ireland, shaping its demographics to such an extent that the population of Ireland still has not returned to pre-famine numbers. The blight had a devastating impact on the Irish people because the poor of the land were so dependent on the potato as their staple food. Exports of other foodstuffs from Ireland, including potatoes, continued right throughout the famine years. It is said, for instance, that exports of all livestock from Ireland to England increased during the famine, except for pigs, although exports of ham and bacon did increase. *An Gorta Mór* was the result of deliberate economic and political policy decisions in Westminster.

The already strained relationship with the British Crown also worsened during these years, sectarian and ethnic tensions were stirred and the increasing diaspora, particularly in the United States, helped seed the growing threat of violence against British rule in Ireland. Stories survive of Protestant clergy establishing soup kitchens to feed those displaced from the land, who were mostly Catholic. In some cases, food was only provided on the condition that they converted to Protestantism, and those who did became known as 'Soupers', or those who 'took the soup'. The term continues to live on in the vernacular for someone who is disloyal or who changes allegiance.

All this is to say that being turned away during hungry

times is not an experience easily forgotten or laid aside. Antagonism towards the Moabites has a lasting, generational sting, so much so in fact that it was enshrined in the Law of Moses. In Deuteronomy 23 the Law states that an Egyptian, whose nation had enslaved Israel for centuries, could be forgiven and the third generation of their children could be considered one of the people of God (Deut. 23.7–8). Moabites, however, were altogether different. They should never, ever be admitted to the people of God, not even if over ten generations they prove themselves faithful. The clear reason given is because when the Israelites were hungry and thirsty the Moabites did not meet that need with bread and water (Deut. 23.3–4).

So when a story opens with a famine and a flight to Moab, then the original audience is primed for the same response. It stirs the ancient antipathy that lies only barely below the surface of polite human interaction during the days when things could be considered stable. The storyteller knows that the old stereotypes of mean and tight-fisted Moabites could be relied on to anticipate a certain unfolding of the story, for only a fool would flee to Moab during a great hunger. Everyone thinks they know how this story will end.

This sense of inevitability is heightened by a second detail in the opening paragraph of the narrative. After Elimelech's tragic death, Naomi foolishly, in the opinion of the original receivers perhaps, allows her two sons to marry Moabite women. Once again there is a familiar trope being pursued here. The tradition says that Moabite women are famously unreliable. This trope is buried deep in the Torah, in Numbers 25, where a story is told of sexually voracious Moabite women who lead poor innocent Israelite men astray. The account tells that ultimately 24,000 people died in a plague that afflicted the people because of the Lord's anger at their sin with these women. The text is unambiguous and goes on to say that the Moabite women, with whom the men had had illicit sex, also enticed these men into worshipping foreign gods.

If fleeing Bethlehem in a famine to go to Moab was one foolish act, it is compounded by this second. Marrying these boys to Moabite women can only end in heartbreak because – in the stereotypes of the story-world being explored – there is no way these scheming, manipulative Moabite women can remain faithful. Sure enough, death comes. And once again the storyteller can anticipate a predictable response: marry a Moabite woman and have your heart broken, at best.

And now Naomi is left without husband or sons, and everyone knows how the rest of this story will unfold.

On the back foot

What is astonishing about the narrative is that all this drama occurs in just the opening five verses. Famine, flight, death, marriages and more deaths; this is more than enough drama for several volumes, and yet the storyteller seems anxious to move through it all with some pace, as if it is the backdrop to what follows. And of course it is. The hearer, or reader, has been set up to expect a certain outcome to the search for hospitality in Moab and the all-too-human desire for companionship with Moabite women, but what follows in the rest of the story defies every stereotype these people, presumably Israelites or Judahites, have of Moabites. Indeed, it may even be that the whole purpose of the book is to unpick the ancient stereotypes of Moabites so deeply woven into the fabric of history, tradition and experience of the people of Judah. Such a self-examination preserved in sacred text is a wondrous call: so often in contemporary politics, we see that voices of self-examination are derided as being unpatriotic. In the Hebrew Bible, self-examination through stories that upset stereotypes is praised as the practice of virtue.

The book of Ruth begins a process of challenging stereotypes by inviting the hearer or reader to consider the possibility of a new story in the relationship between these peoples. In the beginning, beleaguered and embittered Bethlehemites in the face of a famine might perceive Moab as the proper place for mean, tight-fisted Elimelech, and that his children deserve Moabite women. But as the story proceeds, the reader must face the uncomfortable prospect that Moab welcomes the family, and the widow Naomi finds a lasting home there for at least ten years (Ruth 1.4). Her sons also find wives, who continue to care for their mother-in-law even after the deaths of their husbands, when tradition would dictate that their marriage contracts had ended. By not leaving Naomi when they were entitled to and, by implication, not demanding back the dowry their fathers had paid, which they were also entitled to do, they are acting as if their marriage contracts were still in effect.

Naomi has to plead with them to leave her and only then does Orpah turn around and go home. Ruth, however, professes deep loyalty and commitment to her widowed mother-in-law in language that remains profoundly moving even today (1.16–17). Nobody in the orbit of this story would have expected this outcome. Hospitable Moabites didn't exist. Faithful and good Moabite women were unknown, but here the audience was been invited to consider the possibility that their inherited assumptions might be wrong and that change was possible.

The practice of stereotyping

We stereotype a people group when we apply to them a fixed and generalized set of beliefs about them. In some ways it seems inevitable in that it enables us to respond quickly to certain situations because we are able to apply the benefit of select prior experience. Where stereotyping becomes dangerous is when we ignore differences between individuals in that people group. Stereotypes simplify our social world and reduce the amount of data we have to process about our social interactions. It is easier to say that all Moabites lack generosity, or all British people want to dominate Irish people, or all Mexicans want to take advantage of American prosperity, rather than deal with the complexity of the individual standing before us. In stereotyping, we infer that that individual has the characteristics we already assumed all members of their group have. Negative stereotyping leads us into prejudice and assumptions about intention; *we* have suffered and *they* intended it to happen, therefore it is their fault. Writing as a white man, I see my words about stereotyping to be important for my own self-reflection, learning and repentance, demonstrated in changed behaviours and in challenging others who look like me in the stereotypes they hold that are operational in Irish culture, tacitly and explicitly.

When we get caught up in the negative circle of blame it becomes too easy to separate into in-groups and out-groups and to believe then that everything that benefits them harms us and vice versa. This has the effect of reinforcing negative group identity and loyalty because any attempt to justify 'their' actions or criticize 'our' behaviour is seen as treasonous. In such situations, empathy for the 'other' is impossible and dialogue with them is dangerous. Violence against them becomes a self-fulfilling prophecy; their perceived antipathy towards us makes hostility towards them permissible and sometimes even desirable in order to maintain or establish the status quo.

It is significant that in this narrative attempt to address the stereotypes of Moabites the audience is not asked to change their minds about a whole people group. Instead they are asked to consider the possibility of one good, loyal, hard-working Moabite woman. Boaz thus draws attention to her loyalty and care for Naomi, and witnesses to the public knowledge of her good character (2.11–12; 3.10–11). The women of the town attest to something similar (4.15). Most intriguingly of all perhaps, even Boaz's land manager, who can't get beyond the racial stereotype and who on one occasion calls her 'Ruth the Moabite from Moab' (2.6), must confess that she is polite and hard-working (2.7). It is clear that although in the first two chapters Ruth is rarely mentioned without reference to her ethnicity, the people of Bethlehem are having to redraw their general idea of Moabites. By her actions, the window into her people changes. That she had to 'prove' her virtue is a complex burden, one that will be explored later.

The final evidence that the stereotypes have been undermined and a new understanding of community created is the inclusion of the family line of Perez at the very end of the book (4.18–22). While the stated purpose of Boaz's intended marriage to Ruth was to preserve the family line of Mahlon (Ruth's deceased first husband), and through him the memory of Elimelech (4.5), the final list of names attached at the end of the text makes no mention of Mahlon at all, though Boaz is included. Perhaps more significantly still, we must reckon with the uncomfortable fact that the future great King David has a Moabite in his bloodline. Relationships have been so redrawn and extended that they include a foreigner even in the royal line.

Conclusion

The book of Ruth is so much more than consolation after the book of Judges, and not simply a quaint love story. It is in fact a sophisticated work of inter-cultural awareness. It displays a complex understanding of how in certain circumstances there is no such thing as the past, rather there is a history that continues to play itself out in our present unless we make a conscious effort to address the pain and trauma that we experienced and have caused. Thus Ireland needs to unpick and understand its persistent preoccupation with Britain (England in particular), and recognize an interdependence. And Britain must come to terms with its colonial past and resist its imagined victimhood at the hands of the European Union. If these islands are to move to anything resembling a healthy future, we must deal urgently with our living history and stop pretending that it is our past.

The book of Ruth is also a radical theological act. It recognizes that the national stereotype of Moabites is overcome by a new story; indeed, it is an acknowledgement that new stories are always possible. And these new stories are not told on the level of nation states or whole people groups but through personal and human encounter. In this way the book demonstrates the enduring and transforming power of incarnation.

Sawubona is a common greeting in Zulu. It can be translated as 'I see you; you are valued by me, and I acknowledge your full humanity'. The traditional response is *Shiboka* which means 'I exist for you'. At the root of so much of our conflict and disagreement is our inability, or our refusal, to genuinely see and take note of the full humanity of another person. In this Zulu greeting and response the full humanity of the individual is acknowledged in all their virtues and their flaws. The Benedictines have a practice that is somewhat similar. The monastic bow by which a monk greets another person is an acknowledgement of the humanity of that person as one in whom the image of God dwells. It also orientates the monk's head to the earth, thereby grounding them and helping them recognize that the person they now welcome shares the same place and the same feet of clay. Only such radical generosity can overcome our destructive stereotypes and prejudices and create new possibilities for relationship, and in these new relationships, new nation-making in our policies and practices towards each other.

4

The Second Act of the Book of Ruth

PÁDRAIG Ó TUAMA

I once had to take part in an interview for a course in Conflict Mediation. It was the most peculiar interview I have ever experienced. I was paired up with someone called Maggie – we bonded over bewilderment and immediate mutual liking – and we were sent into a room where an Albanian official (really it was a man called Seán) spoke to us in a foreign language and we were told to plead for our safety as newly landed refugees.

Seán – or his Albanian alter persona – spoke back to us in a language neither of us understood. Maggie and I had to get to know each other very quickly (we decided that we were married; hard times call out strange heteronormative behaviours in me) and find out how to negotiate. Seán tried to split us up, but our recent marriage was, it seems, a loyal one, and we insisted we would not be put in different rooms. The whole interview – God almighty, it lasted almost two hours – was designed to put us in situations of stress, confusion, anxiety, and (I think) call out fortitudes and supportive behaviours. Both Maggie and I got on to the course. Neither of us knew why, and were both afraid to ask.

Every time I see Seán now, I think of him as an Albanian

who speaks with an Irish accent. One of the lessons I learned on the course was how *not* to conduct an interview. For a brief instant, in a made-up situation, I was confused, bewildered, and trying to mime words and second-guess what asylum-friendly policies might be in place that I could depend on. I think it was designed to say, 'This is a little bit of what it's really like.' But here's the thing: it was nothing like what it's really like. Nothing of that pretend two hours could prepare anyone for imagining what it'd actually be like. What would a person bring in a bag if they could only take one small bag? Who should be designated to carry whom should something terrible happen? Can you plan for such devastations? If we have to choose who lives and who doesn't, how do we choose? How long would the journey be? Food, or a second pair of shoes? Money? Or bargaining chips? Disguise yourself or stand out? Read up on asylum policies or listen to stories that filter back? Would you speak? Would you be silent?

In the second chapter of Ruth, Naomi is mostly silent, although noticeable in the background. She's mentioned twice and then re-enters the narrative at the end once Ruth has established the connection with Boaz. This silence of Naomi – or, to give her the name she had chosen when she arrived back in Bethlehem, Mara – always strikes me. Having been married to a wealthy man who fled a region in distress, she had established her life with her husband and sons in Moab, an unknown territory. The sons married Moabite women, and now all the links to her homeland were dead. Did she want to leave Bethlehem in the first place? Did she resent having to return? How much of her renaming of herself on her arrival back was a performance of shame: shame at having left, and shame now at how poorly everything had worked out for her? That she is mostly silent for this second act seems apposite. She is sitting in the grief of what she's lost and all that this means, rather than in any way being able to mark her survival.

While we conducted 'Ruth and Brexit' groups all across Ireland and Britain, we heard many stories. In one group, a woman – Judith – said that her father had died the year before. Judith is one of five children and each of these five children have children of their own, and some of those children have children themselves. So Judith's parents had children, grandchildren and some great-grandchildren. A few days after the funeral there was a big family gathering – everyone attended. It was a house filled with people – noise and chatter and story and sadness and gladness at a life well lived. Judith's mother, surrounded by generations who loved her, looked at her children and said, 'I have no one in my life now.' Judith told the group this story, saying she was tempted to say, 'Mam, look around, count the generations', but she didn't. She didn't because she took a breath and realized that her mother was telling something true for that moment. Judith recalled this during a session at which we explored the story of Naomi. 'We need to mourn what we've lost before we can see what we still have', she said. And I have never forgotten this. This is true, too, for Naomi, and it is also true for regions of profound conflict. Change brings grief because the past – complicated as it was – has ended, and something new is emerging.

While Naomi is shrouded in these verses of silence, Ruth is the provider for this small family affected by famine and migration. It is Ruth – the stranger in the land – who goes out to test the social welfare provisions of her new country; she who was the wife of a dead local. Or, at least, she who considers herself the wife of the dead Israelite, because there's a complication. The animosity between Moabites and Israelites meant that marriages between people from those regions were taboo and thus unrecognized. Ruth, a widow, is hoping that the provision for widows and orphans will apply to her, the very validity of whose marriage – and therefore widowhood – is a matter of political and sectarian opinion.

It's noted that a marriage between an Israelite woman and a Moabite man was utterly rejected; but a marriage between an Israelite man and a Moabite woman was – in theory at least – acknowledged as being valid. However, that was in theory alone: no such marriage had, until Ruth's story, been recognized. Ruth finds herself at the hinge of so many laws. She is the hinge-point as to whether such a despised marriage would be acknowledged as a marriage, even though death has separated them. A man at one of our events told us that after his partner died, he had great difficulty persuading the church authorities to permit him to have 'beloved partner' on the gravestone, as the church did not want to acknowledge the dead man had a male partner. They proposed the word 'friend' instead. The bereaved partner won out in the end, but having to fight this battle was exhausting when he was already worn out by grief. Language is a power, and the powers set up around the languages of love are armed indeed.

Ruth finds herself at the hinge of some other laws too – whether she is able to marry someone else in the family other than the man who might have been considered under law to 'own' her, as the wife of his dead kinsman. Ruth is a matriarch for people who are the *firsts*: the first person of a particular ethnicity or nationality to claim an entitlement, to be in public, to get a payment, to enact their own life as they see fit. Being the first is both trying and tiring. Ruth is the first Moabite to benefit from the somewhat complicated law that permitted Moabite women to marry into Israelite families but not Moabite men. Small beginnings are rarely perfect and always problematic. Ruth opens the door.[1]

All eyes were on her, and not only because of her projected sexualizing, due to her nationality. All eyes were on her to watch how she behaved. Did she act as though she deserved what she was getting? Did she act superior to the others out gleaning the corners of the field? Did she speak too much about her dead husband? Or too little? Did she act overly familiar with someone? Or was she standoffish? Did she speak too much? Or too little?

Ruth finds herself safe in the field of Boaz, gleaning among the others who need access to this provision. The practice of leaving the corners of a field unharvested in order to provide for widows and orphans is a beautiful practice, known as the Laws of the Field:

> When you reap the harvest of your land, you shall not reap to the very edges of your field, or gather the gleanings of your harvest. You shall not strip your vineyard bare, or gather the fallen grapes of your vineyard; you shall leave them for the poor and the alien: I am the LORD your God. (Lev. 19.9–10)

Ruth is both poor and an alien, but it seems that even provisions for the poor and the alien are disputed. Are you the right kind of poor or the right kind of foreigner? Was your marriage to the dead local the kind of marriage that is approved of? Why are you here? What are your intentions? These questions hovered around her – and many today – like vultures.

---

1 Avivah Zornberg, *The Murmuring Deep* (New York: Schocken Books, 2009), p. 360.

At this stage Boaz is introduced properly. He has been mentioned as a relative of Naomi's but now he walks the field as if it were a stage. He is introduced graciously: he greets the reapers and they answer with equal courtesy. Then he asks, referring to Ruth, 'To whom does this young woman belong?' Ruth, it seems, takes everybody's attention, because of her nationality, reputation and her actions towards her mother-in-law. Were this an actual play, there might be music when Boaz sees Ruth and asks about her; asks – in the English renderings anyway – to whom she *belongs*. Is he asking what family she is from? Or this is an assumption of indentured servitude? And why is Boaz so taken with her? And who is Boaz anyway? Who is he when he's at home? The Midrash would have us understand that Ruth and Naomi arrived back in Bethlehem while Boaz's wife was being buried. He is not spoken of as being a person in grief, or a parent yet. Is it that a widowed person recognizes the shared experience resting on another? Ruth's presence is magnetic, although in Boaz's gaze at least, the attention does not seem to be predatory but rather the opposite.

Boaz has asked his servant about Ruth and the servant speaks of her as having worked all day, having remained on her feet. Speaking to Ruth, then, Boaz instructs her to remain close to his young women, and furthermore he tells her that he has 'ordered the young men not to bother you' (2.9). The JPS (Jewish Publication Society – Jewish Bible) version renders it like this: 'Have I not charged the young men that they shall not touch thee?'

I try to locate myself in the story-world of this text, and I see that the fields are not uniform but are undulating; they do not have neat corners, but I see corners that are part of copses and crannies. To harvest a corner is to be out of sight, which can be a treat or a threat. The corners that are untended are also the corners where hidden things can happen. Like so many people who have fled famine and crossed borders, Ruth knows that to provide for her family is to put her own body at risk. She is out there anyway. She has found her way to a field where someone sees her for the person she is – her capacities and actions – rather than a piece of foreign female meat. 'Stay close to the young women', and 'I have ordered my men not to bother you.' The word translated as 'bother' or 'touch' here is curious. It is *naga* – and it occurs elsewhere in the Hebrew Bible too

Adam and Eve are told not to *touch* the forbidden fruit.

God *afflicts* the house of the Pharaoh with great plagues.

Jacob dreams of a ladder *reaching* towards heaven.

The Angel of God *strikes* Jacob in the hip socket, causing him to limp.

The lintels of the Hebrews, during the stay in Egypt, were *touched* with blood to save the people from the Angel of Death.

The text of Leviticus speaks over and over again of things a person should *touch* and things a person should not *touch*.

And Job asks his friends for pity because the hand of God has *touched* him.

To touch is to impact: to strike, to afflict, to plague, to cause transfer, to make holy or unholy. How often the dignity of touch is violated. Negative touch is a brutal spectrum that ranges from the annihilating to the unreported, to the unpleasant, to the unasked for. The question of touch is one that holds the story of Ruth and Boaz throughout the narrative, and here we see that touch is a privilege, not assumed. If many have fantasized about Ruth, taking liberties in their imaginations, Boaz's imagination seems filled with knowledge of her kindness to Naomi, and for this he honours her. Ruth wonders why she has earned the favour, and Boaz speaks of the story that we all know. He invites her to eat his bread, and when Ruth returns to Naomi, Naomi tells her to continue gleaning in the field and says of Boaz, 'The man is a relative of ours, one of our nearest kin' (2.20).

Rather than a simple fact, this is a piece of golden information. Naomi has been shown to be a woman who honours obligation. When both of her sons died, she lamented:

> Turn back, my daughters, go your way, for I am too old to have a husband. Even if I thought there was hope for me, even if I should have a husband tonight and bear sons, would you then wait until they were grown? (Ruth 1.12–13)

By marrying, Naomi's sons and, by association, the entire family, had taken on an obligation to provide for Orpah and Ruth. Now, after the death of Naomi's sons, Orpah and Ruth are childless widows and Naomi is aware that her side of the family has not fulfilled its obligations. What are the decorums of devastation? When a border-crossing family arrives, what indignities have they suffered, in body, spirit, obligation and culture? Naomi seems broken both by grief as well as by being unable to provide for these two Moabite women whose people have become her people.

Ordinarily in these circumstances, one of the nearest male relatives is a potential doorway into an economic obligation. To read the pressure Naomi was under to provide husbands for her daughters-in-law as simple romance is to miss the point of her energy: where others look at Ruth and see 'just a Moabite', Naomi sees her and knows that she *owes* her. She doesn't only owe her a great debt of gratitude for accompaniment and provision. To the threat of her own body, Naomi also owes her because she is in her debt. Naomi remembers, and now – with Ruth returned from the field filled with provisions and a story about a benevolent field-owner – sees an opportunity for the redemption of her own reputation as a woman of valour. Naomi's name means 'sweet', but sweetness doesn't taste itself. Sweetness needs to be shared, to be savoured, and she has been unable to share what she is committed to, so has turned bitter. Sugar has soured. But now she sees a way. Naomi's passivity in this second act of the book is soon to change into instruction, insight, scheming and knowledge of the ways of men.

The story of the world is a story of migrating peoples. For millennia, people have moved across seas and over mountain ranges. Empires seized lands and created borders. With borders and empires came the idea of policing the *permission* to move, and the era of Christianist empires introduced the imagination that you only have to be in a country a few hundred years before you become the ones with the *right* to be there, policing other people who are seeking to arrive as your recent forebears did, only a generation – or three or four – before. This book of Ruth is an intervention into the story.

The last few years have seen much discussion about borders and walls, and the threats that newcomers pose to the stability of those who see that their belonging is threatened by a wider table of belonging. Whether that's about building bigger walls or separation walls, or turning boats around or asking where a person is *really* from, we see it everywhere. What do we do with this? The book of Ruth does not tell people how to vote, and nor does it propose a political policy on the question of open borders. But it does paint a recognizable picture: someone has arrived in a foreign country and she is aware of the hostility she is facing. She has obligations, and she is faithful and good and kind to someone she loves who is full of grief. She is not seen for who she is but as the Moabite from Moab.

Your people will be my people, Ruth had promised, and she is true to the promise. But that's only one side. Will *that* people take her as one of *their* people? She has no control over that. And – for a while at least – Naomi is consumed with her own hollowed-out heart. Ruth works harder than locals, at considerable risk to herself, under substantially more threat than locals. Her body is at risk in being out in public, but her status as a migrant, and as a Moabite migrant in particular, puts her under special threat and attention.

In both a personal and political sense, a person needs to be seen. Ruth seeks to be seen. She does not come with threat to the people in this new borderland. She comes with love, but also honesty: she is honest about the truth that she sees herself as belonging, even if others do not.

So she gleaned in the field until evening. Then she beat out what she had gleaned, and it was about an ephah of barley. She picked it up and came into the town, and her mother-in-law saw how much she had gleaned. (2.17–18)

5

Counter-Narratives

GLENN JORDAN

The book of Ruth is unusual in the Bible in that it makes its claim to theological or doctrinal truth through the medium of narrative. With the exception of an explanatory note in Ruth 4.7, there is no didactic material nor are there any instructions delivered directly from God concerning the behaviours of human beings. Instead the reader is expected to do the work of reflection and consideration on the significance of the story. The book is also unusual because its principal characters are women. Even though popular exegesis and sermonic treatments tend to focus on the rescuing work of Boaz, nevertheless the title of the book preserves for us the name of the key actor in the story. A question remains, however, as to why this book should have been preserved in the canon of Scripture for both Jews and Christians. One possible answer is that it emerged in a particular time in the nation's history to address, through narrative, some of the pressing issues of the day.

We have no real certainty about when this book was written or who the author may have been. The traditional view is that Samuel wrote it, and that would certainly account for its placement between Judges and 1 Samuel in the Christian Old Testament. In this view, Ruth is a bridging book setting the scene for the introduction of the kingship in

Israel in the books attributed to Samuel. It opens by setting itself in the era of the judges and ends with the genealogy of David, thereby spanning two critical periods in the development of the nation of Israel. In Judges, the leaders emerge spontaneously and informally, do what work they have to do and then fade back into obscurity. The new era, ushered in by Samuel, leads to the establishment of a formal monarchy. The books of Samuel tell the story of the appointment of Saul as the first leader/king in Israel – a sort of halfway point between the informality of a judge and the establishment of a dynastic monarchy. David succeeds him as a more effective leader and the one who also establishes many of the institutions associated with kingship. Ruth may be considered, in Christian circles at least, as the connecting tissue between these eras, but this still cannot account for the preservation of the book, nor does it answer in any effective way the issue of its dating.

There are, however, technical and linguistic reasons to call into question an early dating for the book, and while Ruth places itself in the era of the judges, the writer is obviously familiar with David, who came much later. That said, it is likely that the story was transmitted orally, perhaps for many centuries, before being written down, quite possibly in the post-exilic period, when the social, economic and political circumstances were such that they called for a story of this kind. This sets up the intriguing possibility that there are occasions in history when the proper response to the times is not another war or new legislation, not even an election, but a work of art. In this case, the process of gathering an oral account and committing it to writing stands in front of the juggernaut of history in an attempt to divert the hearts of people towards some lasting values, and to remind them of their better selves.

47

In the run-up to the October 2019 deadline for Brexit, I found myself wearying of the news, which sought, through the bawl of headlines, to tell me what was really important. It seemed to me at the time to be an endless succession of raised voices, from all sides of the debate, telling me why this one and that one was not speaking the truth. Meanwhile, behind these dominating voices there were many issues deemed not so important but which were matters of life and death to many. As the debate ebbed and flowed, and positions seemed to dominate then decline only to rise again, it was hard to hold to any sort of equilibrium. Whether winning or losing on any particular question commentators, opinion formers, politicians from all sides and the twitterati just shouted louder and louder until it all formed the background noise of the day. Even for one who has a fascination with politics like me, one voice was indistinguishable from another in the general din.

At the same time, in the United States, President Trump was facing the growing threat of impeachment while simultaneously withdrawing from northern Syria and potentially leaving the way clear for war between Turkey and key US allies the Kurds. This was being condemned even by his supporters. Online, on television and in print, the same babble of voices fought hard to make themselves comprehensible, all competing for a sliver of airspace in which to be heard. Meanwhile, streets of major cities throughout the world resounded with the music of protest songs and beating drums as young people and adults demonstrated against the escalation of our climate crisis, while in Hong Kong young protesters wore masks and were shot at by police as they rebelled against the state for the maintenance of their freedoms.

In each case, competing voices struggled to be heard and resorted to ever more desperate means to make their passions visible. Children went on strike from school; a man chained himself to a hearse; people risked imprisonment and worse by wearing face-coverings; politicians crossed the floor. As the cacophony rises, something truly exceptional is required to cut through the clamour to make an impact on an electorate that has been pummelled into insensibility by the rival voices.

I wonder if Israel's return from exile in Babylon was as similarly fraught as the era in which we find ourselves today. Given our understanding of human nature and of power, we should not be surprised that there were competing analyses for why the exile happened in the first place, and hence competing solutions as to how to restore national pride in its aftermath. It is entirely possible that Jerusalem was as much a bear pit back then as Westminster was in the autumn of 2019. It is even possible to discern some of these competing voices in the text of the Bible itself, because far from hiding this conflict or seeking to harmonize different perspectives, it preserves them for us and invites us into the dialogue for our time and place. For instance, the followers of Jeremiah, the radical prophet from Anathoth, carry on his message that the seeds of their downfall were sown in the establishment of the institution of the monarchy and in the centralization of worship at the temple in Jerusalem. The antidote to the original departure from faithfulness to Yahweh is to dismantle the establishment, topple the throne and return to localized and rural expressions of worship and devotion in defiance of the urban elite.

For the prophet Ezekiel and his followers, the original sin was the defiling of the temple. To make Israel great again, therefore, the nation must restore the purity of their worship and approach to Yahweh. No construction, nor any work of restoration should take place until the temple is restored in all its glory. Those who followed in the tradition of the prophet Isaiah displayed all the passion, intensity and perhaps the bitter disappointment of those who recognized the social injustices that led to the break-up of the nation and their own complicity in it, proposed a new social vision, but who perhaps found that the nation was not likely to embrace this new vision.

And then there was the Ezra and Nehemiah axis. Many scholars have remarked that the book of Ruth may be a reaction to the measures that Ezra and Nehemiah took during their period in charge in Jerusalem after the return from exile. Of course, this remains a source of much debate in scholarly literature and it is something hard to prove definitively, but even the fact that this book has been preserved in the canon over many centuries for both Jews and Christians, and exists alongside Ezra and Nehemiah, should give careful readers reason to pause.

Ezra, Nehemiah and foreigners

Both Ezra and Nehemiah are concerned for the physical state of the city of Jerusalem and also the spiritual health of the people. The book of Ezra opens with a decree from Cyrus, the king of Persia, which permits those exiled from Judah to return home and to rebuild their temple (Ezra 1.1–4). The names and family connections of those who choose to go back are preserved in a long list, indicating that bloodlines remain important even in the trauma of conquest. Very soon after the return the sacrificial system is reinstated and the rebuilding of the temple commences despite considerable opposition from their enemies. On completion of the work, however, the whole mechanism of priests and Levites was reinstated, sacrifices were offered and the people worshipped at the temple as they did in the time before destruction overtook them.

It also became clear during this time that bad practices had taken root during the period of exile, and even the priests and Levites were guilty of misbehaviour, namely that they had not kept separate from the nations around them (the Moabites are named): 'For they have taken some of their daughters as wives for themselves and for their sons. Thus the holy seed has mixed itself with the peoples of the lands' (Ezra 9.2). This description of their wrongdoing is frighteningly contemporary. It is too much for Ezra, who preaches a fiery sermon against this apostasy during evening worship. Convicted by Ezra's words, a man named Shecaniah calls on the assembled people to take a vow before God, 'to send away all these wives and their children' (Ezra 10.3) in obedience to Ezra's admonition. In a strikingly dramatic scene, all the men of Judah and Benjamin are ordered to assemble in the square in front of the temple or face impoverishment. They do so within three days, under torrential rain, and the command is given to separate from their foreign wives (Ezra 10.9–11). A commission of inquiry is established to investigate individual cases and the book of Ezra closes with a permanent record of names of those who had married foreign women.

The book of Nehemiah is a detailed record of the rebuilding of Jerusalem and the opposition it drew from its neighbours. Nehemiah's chief opponent, incidentally, was Sanballat of Horonaim, a city in Moab (Neh. 2.10). This book also records the detailed arrangements made by Ezra for the reading and interpretation of the Law of Moses (Neh. 8), something that presumably hadn't been done since the exile and which led to the rediscovery and celebration of the great feast of Sukkot. Later in the same month it is recorded that they gathered again to worship and read the Law, and curiously the book says they had 'separated themselves from all foreigners' (Neh. 9.2). There is a great liturgical prayer spoken over the people, in which their history with Yahweh is rehearsed and Yahweh is reminded, as if it was needed, of their continued unfaithfulness in the face of Yahweh's gracious compassion. Out of this worship and prayer comes a renewed commitment to purity, expressed in the corporate signing of a vow, with associated curses should they ever fall short. The first principle of the vow is a promise: 'We will not give our daughters to the peoples of the land or take their daughters for our sons' (Neh. 10.30). They follow this with an economic sanction on neighbouring peoples, refusing to buy their merchandise on the Sabbath (Neh. 10.31).

The book ends with Nehemiah's final reforms, which involve a restatement of the earlier command of Moses in Deuteronomy 23.3–6 to prohibit Moabites from ever entering the assembly of God's people. And when the people heard this instruction from Moses, the book records that they 'separated from Israel all those of foreign descent' (Neh. 13.3). The drive for ever greater ritual purity sees the strict implementation of tithes, offerings and of Sabbath observance and, finally, divorce is made mandatory for those men who had married foreign wives. This final edict is enforced with violence (Neh. 13.25), and these forms of marriages are scapegoated as the principal cause of sin and therefore in all likelihood a cause of the exile in the first place (Neh. 13.26–27). The closing words of the book are a plea, even a prayer, that God would remember Nehemiah with favour, presumably because of what he did during his time as leader in Jerusalem.

Perhaps more clearly than any of the great prophets, the books of Ezra and Nehemiah give us some indication of the ferment in Jerusalem and society in general as it came to terms with the impact of conquest, exile and return. When fear and anxiety govern a community's actions in the civic square, there is often a scapegoat created to carry away that community's worst anxieties. And that scapegoat is frequently the stranger. It happened in the Brexit referendum. The possibility of up to 5.2 million people moving to the UK by 2030 under freedom of movement in the EU was successfully manipulated to amplify the Brexit vote. Thus did fear of immigration become one of the defining issues in that vote. Similarly, in the United States, where President Trump labelled a caravan of migrants from Guatemala as 'an invasion' that would overrun the country with a mass of illegal immigrants who would destabilize American society. We should not blithely pass over the Ezra and Nehemiah accounts of growing antagonism towards outsiders when things were tough for indigenous populations, nor the fact that communal fears were stoked into violent actions through the mechanism of mass gatherings. Human nature hasn't changed that substantially, and we do well to read these accounts with wariness and concern.

In recent scholarship the historicity of Ezra and Nehemiah is widely debated, and some believe that, at best, these are the memories, and perhaps interpretative memories, of what happened. And even with those who accept the accounts as written, there are questions about the sequence, the amount of overlap between the two and the dating. However, these debates are not what is of interest here; rather, whether they are accurate accounts or memories, it is the existence of Ezra/Nehemiah and Ruth in the same collection of books that is intriguing.

Ruth as counter-narrative

It is helpful, therefore, to consider the book of Ruth as a counter-narrative to the ideology on display in Ezra and Nehemiah, particularly in relation to the treatment of foreigners in any attempt to define a people group on the basis of ethnic purity. It is also worth considering the form in which this alternative perspective is being presented. An idea is being proposed in the form of a narrative and not another political, historical or sociological argument; that is, an appeal is made to the historical presence of good, loyal and hardworking foreigners, even to the extent of ascribing a foreign bloodline to their greatest king.

In arguing against this view, it might be said that Ruth converted to Judaism and therefore she deserves to be considered as one of their own. Once again, this is a controversial issue in the scholarly literature, because there is no incontrovertible evidence in the text of Ruth's conversion. Did she and Orpah do so on their marriage to the sons? Did she do so at the point of her statement of loyalty to Naomi? Or did she do so on the basis of her marriage to Boaz and the acceptance of this by the people? Set against each of these proposals there are problematic questions that should be posed. When she returns to Bethlehem, she doesn't deny her ethnicity, repeatedly being referred to as the Moabite, nor is there any evidence in the story of Ruth participating in the ritual requirements for conversion. Furthermore, the assertion of loyalty to Naomi is just that – a statement of loyalty to Naomi, which is a prior loyalty even to that afforded to God. And when seen in the light of Ezra/Nehemiah accounts, we should note that no option for conversion appears to be afforded to the women there. Being foreign is merit enough for exclusion. It is worth saying that Jewish tradition skirts this issue in a creative way, in a bid to protect the line of descent of David, by saying that Deuteronomy 23.3 only applies to male and not female Moabites. It is creative but not convincing.

The fact is that Ruth is a foreigner and remains so to the end. Even her eventual disappearance from the story, having provided the heir that Naomi so badly needed, may hint at otherness. And whether this is an ancient song revived and written down as a narrative in the particular context of restoration Judah, or composed specifically for that time and context, the book of Ruth is a contrary voice that stands in stark contrast to the attitudes, behaviours and politics of Ezra/Nehemiah. For these latter characters it seems that imposing divorce on Judahite men who had married foreign women was an essential step on the road back to greatness for the nation, which would henceforth be defined by racial and ritual purity. The task of excluding foreign women and dispossessing them and their children of land is pivotal to defining the nation and consolidating the community in the aftermath of exile and return.

The book of Ruth could therefore reasonably be considered a more complex and radical approach. It could be a counter-narrative making the assertion that ethnic and religious purity was not as important as Ezra and Nehemiah had sought to claim. It might even be opening them, and us, to the possibility that ethnic and religious diversity offers a new approach to nationalism.

Texts in dialogue

It appears that the Bible itself has preserved texts that are in constant dialogue, sometimes even in conflict, with one another. We do well to try and manage this tension rather than try to resolve it by flattening it out into a monotone truth of a single, consistent story. Managing it requires wisdom though, the ability to wrestle with the complexity of ancient and different texts in the context of our own time and history. The book of Ruth comes to us as a counter-narrative to the other, louder and more strategically coherent messages, whether written at the time or in retrospect. That it comes to us by way of narrative and not a manifesto is interesting.

It is interesting because stories have a way of opening up conversation and dialogue by making space for the imagination. In this space new realities can emerge for how things might be different. Storytelling can be a moral response to the kinds of messages that serve to divide peoples, create damaging stereotypes and identify scapegoats. As such, stories can puncture the airtight containers into which we place our truths, bringing both light and oxygen into the space to enliven dialogue and to spark new and previously unimaginable possibilities. It is the role of people of faith to keep alive a storytelling tradition that can play this kind of a role in turbulent times.

The book of Ruth is a quiet but powerful rejoinder to the loud and sometimes strident voices that were active in the turmoil of post-exile Judah. It is feasible that the story was recovered from the oral tradition at a moment when its significance was newly recognized, having previously been lost or forgotten. The theologian Walter Brueggemann speaks of texts that linger in the heritage, perhaps for decades or centuries, only to explode suddenly with new meaning in a new time. If this is the case, then the book encourages us to hunt through the familiar practices of our faith for elements that can help us forge an effective counter-narrative to the divisive and corrosive myths that dominate the public square in our day.

6

The Third Act of the
Book of Ruth

PÁDRAIG Ó TUAMA

What would you do in desperation?

The book of Ruth is not a template for what a strategic plan should look like. It is a story of what people do, in desperate circumstances, with limited options. The Hebrew Bible narratives, while being profoundly moral, do not create a false equivalency between the abstract pure and the embodied complicated. God is the wrestle that is found in the wrestle, not the imagination of the wrestle.

The story of Ruth is not alone in its depiction of people who have had to do desperate things in stretched times. Hagar and Sarah, it seems, did not find their relationship easy; at times Sarah sent Hagar away, and Hagar found herself praying prayers of the almost-dead to the God of those who thought they controlled her. Tamar, the daughter-in-law of Judah, could not have imagined herself pretending to work as a prostitute in order to trick her father-in-law into complying with his legal obligations. Rahab, too, turned against her city in the face of its impending doom and extracted a promise of safety for her and her family. And Bathsheba – she who is almost wordless – has survived the murder of her husband and the death of her son, all because of the actions of a king. Years later, she takes advantage of the decaying king to push her son into kingship, even though he was far from the firstborn.

None of these women were saved by divine intervention. They were saved by their own savvy, pluck, risk and fortitude. Had any of them, I imagine, been asked to design a perfect life for themselves, a life whose circumstances meant they could always depend on the perfectly pure option, they would not have designed the lives they had. Had any of them been asked to narrate the actions of a saving God, a saving religion or a saving community, they would not have narrated such a God, religion or community as we find in their stories. What we are left with is a series of stories of people whose circumstances reflected how foreigners, women and those whose bodies are considered irrelevant are often left to their own devices. And the Hebrew Bible is both brilliant and brutal in its description of how those people – often women – navigated their way through obstacles. These are not abstract stories of and for the pure. These are stories of survival.

Ruth, then, is in a line of narrative matriarchs whose company I imagine she would have both recognized and welcomed. For her, politics, law and religion are all carried in the body, enacted in the body and demonstrated in the body: her own and those of the people she adopted as her own. She belongs. Not because of blood, or even marriage, but because of behaviour.

One time, a man came to see me in deep distress. He was a stranger, and he turned up to a place of complete strangers to ask for help. He was gay – I sensed this as soon as I saw him – and he was petrified to tell me he was gay. I was working in a church-related job, so he'd seen a sign and decided this was his moment of disclosure: to a stranger, someone he'd never see again. After he'd told me (his body was shaking), he pleaded with me to tell him whether, when I met him, I had any inkling he was gay. He said he couldn't cope if he thought that people would guess he was gay. He said that if I'd wondered about his sexuality, I should tell him what alerted me to this wondering, and then he'd work hard to eradicate anything that would give such hints to others in his future. I knew I'd never see him again. I knew I wouldn't be there for him that evening or the next day or the day after or a year from that day. So I lied. I told him that I didn't know what he was going to talk about. He relaxed. I asked some more questions about his safety. I gave him the number of an organization that would help him and a church that wouldn't hate him. For him, the reality of his sexual desire was tearing him apart. He had an understanding of a God who couldn't contemplate the sexual and social reality he lived in, so he sought to alienate himself from his sexual and social truths, to the detriment of his own safety. I couldn't sleep that night. The abstract imaginations of faith are often that: abstract. Then there are the events that happen, and we wonder what kind of verb God is, stretching and conjugating in the circumstances of desperation. I have no resolution about that man. I wonder how he is. I had no easy answers. He had asked me to tell him one kind of truth and I told him another. I did what I thought might work to keep him alive. I prayed: to God, and to the women whose stories are the stories of God. I raged too: at evil and hatred and the forces that destroy dignity while idolizing their own purity. The stories of God we receive through sacred text are often of those who dared stretch the meaning of God into the terrible circumstances they were surviving. Trying to do that today is no less urgent.

Ruth and Naomi are in discussion. Act 2 of the book has demonstrated Boaz – almost the nearest kinsman of this small family – to be a man of valour. Or perhaps he's a man who has a hope of a connection; either is fine. Ruth and Naomi wish to make a plan.

Before Naomi gives Ruth some instructions, we hear some moving words from her: 'My daughter, I need to seek some security for you, so that it may be well with you' (Ruth 3.1).

These, after all this time, seem to be the words of reply to Ruth's famous words: 'Where you go, I will go ...'. Naomi has been struck with the bitterness of grief, of disappointment, of shame, of legal and financial incapacity to follow through on her family's obligations. But now she sees a way. For Naomi, in this moment, love and law are mutually supportive. There is love in the words: 'my daughter'; there is obligation in the words: 'I need'; there is law in the words: 'security for you'. Here is a sentence from the mouth of the returned widowed migrant, whose life has been affected by famine and desperation. She embodies the truth that Law is not torn between life and love. Embodiment is the form that Law seeks: to be shown in the relationship between peoples, even strangers, even border-crossers. So Naomi seeks to support Ruth in establishing safety and a future for herself.

She instructs Ruth to anoint herself, put on her best clothes and wait until the men have finished drinking before making herself known to Boaz.

Ruth anoints herself, goes to the threshing floor and uncovers the feet of Boaz.

Did Ruth and Boaz have sex that night? Much is suggested in the text, and much is made in the literature – both ancient and contemporary – of this question. Many also question whether Naomi, by instructing Ruth, was some kind of matriarchal pimp.

Behind all these questions (and, as a spoiler alert, I think that the questions are more interesting than the answers), is a perspective on sex. Did Ruth have sex with Boaz? So what if she did. Did Naomi and Ruth concoct a way in which the power of sex helped seal a deal? So what if they did. (Yesterday I saw a poster for a Christian event in Belfast, a poster that showed some extraordinarily good-looking men at prayer. Sex has been selling in religion and out of religion for as long as there's been religion.) In the Midrash, Ruth's first anxiety seems to be the question of her safety rather than her so-called purity, as highlighted in this conversation with Naomi:

> 'And it shall be, when he lies down, that you will mark the place where he shall lie, and you will go in, and uncover his feet, and lay down; and he will tell thee what you will do.' And she said unto her: 'All that thou say unto me I will do.' Ruth said to [Naomi]: 'What if one from the dogs should come and rape me?' (Ruth Rabbah, chapter 5)

In stories of displacement today, and in stories of displacement for years, women have wondered what men – God, we can be worse than dogs – will do to them along the way.

Marriage came with much obligation: money, protection, land, inheritance and – this is a complicated word – ownership. For centuries, women wore the rings that men gave them as a sign of being owned by men. These days spouses exchange rings with each other, in a sign of mutuality, and others make the moral choice to distance themselves from marriage – an institution too long associated with imaginations of dominance, perhaps – and live out loving partnerships without reference to old practices they find distasteful. There are many shapes that make a partnership loving.

In some of the gatherings we held exploring Brexit and the book of Ruth, the folks who attended said that if Ruth and Boaz had sex before they were married then the morality of both was sullied, thus the message of the book was less clear. In this imagination, it seemed to me that Ruth, in order to be 'acceptable', needed to pass certain purity standards to be considered the right type of Moabite. Whose standards? And what would the problem have been had they had sex that night? Would it have meant that one or the other of them were 'spoiled'? Would it have been a breaking of the law that dictated that Ruth should – by right – have been offered to the nearer kinsman in the family of her dead husband? What is the association with marriage and sex and holiness? Is all sex in marriage holy? Is all sex outside marriage unholy? Both Boaz and Ruth were previously married: Ruth to Naomi's son and Boaz to the woman who was being buried the day that Ruth arrived back with her mother-in-law. They have each, we imagine, been in the arms of another, so it's not as though they are wrecking the imagination of The One.

Some of the speculation about whether they had sex comes from the word 'feet'. This is feet as in 'things with toes' as opposed to 'size matters'. In the Hebrew Bible, the word 'feet' (*regel*) is, at times, a euphemism for genitals. In 2 Samuel 11.8, David instructs Uriah to have sex with Bathsheba and says, 'Go down to your house and wash your feet.' The afterbirth is described as coming out from between a woman's feet (Deut. 28.57). Other texts too – Exodus 4.25; Judges 5.27; 1 Samuel 24.3; 2 Kings 18.27; and Ezekiel 16.25 – could be interpreted through this euphemistic light. The angels described in the sixth chapter of Isaiah are covering their feet with two of their six wings. Some scholars suggest that this is implying that the Seraphim's wings were covering up their genitals. So returning to Ruth, the word 'feet' itself does not definitely imply the word penis in this narrative, but the erotic charge of the chapter is undeniable, whatever is understood about the actions and outcomes of that night.

The Midrash is at pains to communicate that Ruth and Boaz did not have sex. Rabbi Chunya, Jeremiah, Samuel and Yitzchak all seem to be of a mind. They speak in the voice of Boaz:

> All that very night Boaz was prostrated in prayer on his face, saying: 'Master of Worlds, let it be revealed and known before you that I did not touch her, and so may it be your will that it not be known that the woman came to the threshing-floor and the name of Heaven not be desecrated because of me. (Ruth Rabbah, chapter 7)

This question, however, is still rather problematic. If they had sex, would their lives have been poisoned? Or would their hope for a modified Levirate marriage be rendered invalid? The morning after, Ruth awakens Boaz. He gives her six measures of barley to bring back to Naomi, on her back. This posture – said to be the posture of a man carrying a crop – is perhaps a disguise. Others have suggested that giving her seeded grain to carry is a literary device for implying she had conceived that night. Which is true? Which do we need to be true? Would the reputation of Ruth and Boaz suffer if it seemed they consummated that night? Or would it be the reputation of Ruth that suffers more than that of Boaz? Why is it that women's purity is more of a topic for public discussion than men's? And why, when discussing matters of borders, belonging, politics and law, do groups become so interested in sex and purity? So often, public comment moves from serious questions of policy to the question of *deserving*. Does this particular border-crosser *deserve* inclusion? If yes, why? If no, why? Who sets the standards for deserving, and is the deserving a way of maintaining power over-and-above another? If so, can it be imagined in another way?

The way we imagine purity says a lot about the way we imagine other things. The gendered and sexed and embodied rules we have regarding virginity – not to mention the associations between virginity and purity – have been powerful and overwhelming for many populations, notably females, for millennia. By asking Ruth to at least bring herself to the site where sex could happen, Naomi has suggested to Ruth that she enact a Moabite stereotype. Moabites seemed to think of Israelite men as aggressive; Israelites tended to speak of Moabite women as loose. The story told by the Israelites of the origins of the Moabites was that Lot's older daughter got Lot drunk and slept with him, conceiving, and giving birth to Moab.

This is repeated elsewhere – in the Midrash, Rabbi Chanina said, 'the arrogance of Moab was not for the name of Heaven but for the name of promiscuity' (Ruth Rabbah, chapter 5). One of the objections to this text is whether Naomi acted as a pimp. While Ruth's and Naomi's circumstances were not, I imagine, what they imagined for their lives, I do not see that they were establishing an enterprise that would continue beyond a hopefully successful seduction of Boaz, even an unconsummated seduction. Naomi is certainly giving her foreign daughter-in-law instructions about how to bring Boaz to the point of dedication. These are desperate times. Their lives and livelihoods are at stake. They need to become associated to another through marriage. They are saving each other. This is not a denial of purity, this is a practice of self-determination. It highlights once again the morals of the story: the things Ruth and Naomi had to do to find safety and a home highlighted the laws that were in need of change. Their own behaviours – even if they did engage in planning sex to ensure safety – are not depicted by the narrative as scandal. The true scandal in this story is the experience of the border-crossers.

Those who oppose border-crossing have often hidden their objection to that in the seemingly innocent conversation about what constitutes a *deserving* person. Do we think they are kind? Do they sound like us? Do they act according to our laws of purity? Can they assimilate well with us? Do they fit in without causing us a fuss? In all of these, it is the pronouns that are worth recording: we; they; they; us; they; our; they; us; they; us. The real question is the imagination of humanity; the scandal is the assessment of foreign purity.

To return to the text, we can consider Boaz's experience of the night. He seems shocked when he awakes at midnight: 'the man was startled and turned over, and there, lying at his feet, was a woman!' (Ruth 3.8).

Other translations render the word 'startled' differently: Robert Alter translates it as 'trembled and twisted round'. The word itself appears elsewhere to describe Isaac trembling (Gen. 27.33), Mount Sinai shaking violently (Ex. 19.18), panic (Judg. 8.12) and terror (Zech. 1.21). Why would Boaz be so frightened? Perhaps it's as simple as being awoken from a deep, wine-induced sleep. But underneath this is a story of contrast. Ruth, who has so much to fear, in the present and in her future, is depicted as being in control of herself and putting herself at great peril in order to secure a future for herself and Naomi. Boaz is terrified. In all of this text, Ruth is the protagonist. She is the saving actor in this narrative: saving herself, Naomi and – through Boaz – offering a new way of imagining belonging to the community.

By doing what she does, Ruth is, in effect, proposing marriage. She asks Boaz to spread his cloak, a phrase reminiscent of establishing kinship and safety:

I passed by you again and looked on you; you were at the age for love. I spread the edge of my cloak over you, and covered your nakedness: I pledged myself to you and entered into a covenant with you, says the Lord GOD, and you became mine. (Ezek. 16.8)

Ruth and Naomi are two women schooled in the ways of surviving in a world of men. They are demonstrating resilience, fortitude and determination by being leaders of their shared life. Not only this, Ruth the Moabite from Moab is seen as an image of God, seeking cover from a people not her own, and bringing them into the shelter of her kindness, while she trusts that they will bring her into the shelter of theirs. She covenants herself to them in a way that brings about her own redemption, and theirs; both through politics and lovingkindness.

7

Compassion and the Law

GLENN JORDAN

The book of Ruth posits a compelling idea to address the painful and isolating realities of social division and its impact on the common good. And the core of the idea is a word that occurs frequently throughout the text, which in Hebrew is *chesed*; generally translated as 'lovingkindness' and probably the nearest thing in Hebrew to the Christian understanding of the word 'grace'. In two years of working with Ruth, and listening to the story with others as it does its work among us, I have come to think that this small book may be one of the most radical in the whole of the Bible. In large part these conversations we've been having throughout Ireland and Britain on the issue of borders and belonging have circled round the need to establish the idea and the practice of kindness as a critical element in our civic dialogue on contentious matters.

Earlier in the discussion of the liturgical use of Ruth we considered the possibility that the kindnesses in the story may be the appropriate interpretative lens through which to view the Torah, or the Law of Moses, but at that time we didn't consider what the outcome might be of using this particular lens. Now is that moment, for Ruth brings us to a point of decision about how the Bible itself works when it intersects with lived experience.

The wealthy character Boaz is eventually compelled to action by the overwhelming and simple kindnesses of Ruth, the foreigner in the story. He, along with the whole neighbourhood, has seen Ruth's enduring goodness towards the poor widow Naomi, her mother-in-law and one of their own. On this basis, then, Boaz urges the population to accept Ruth as a local for the purposes of social protection and for inclusion as a full member of the community.

By the final chapter, Boaz challenges the townspeople to recognize that though the Law has no formal protection for a foreigner like Ruth, and more particularly for a Moabite foreigner, surely this could be considered an unintended oversight. And so he persuades the residents of Bethlehem to extend the full protections of the Law to this outsider. In effect Ruth becomes a member of the people of God, she becomes kin, on the basis of her kindnesses rather than her ethnicity. It raises the prospect for us, therefore, that belonging can come in a variety of ways, and that our call as Christians is towards kindness as the fullest possible completion of the Law and tradition. This is a deceptively simple calling, because it seems all too easy and naive in the face of the complexities of the hard divisions of Brexit, or those between the bordered parts of Ireland.

How can kindness navigate a way through our traditional divides here? How can kindness plot a course through Brexit?

Considering kindness

The Hebrew word for famine is *ra'av* and it can signify more than just the absence of food; it can also speak for an absence of morals, a distance from God or a lack of kindness. A part of the literary scandal of the opening of the book of Ruth is that this family flees to the place of their traditional enemies. By the time of the journey, the antagonism on Judah's part has been around for generations, rooted in Moab's lack of hospitality when the children of Israel were in the wilderness. As a consequence of this lack of kindness, Moab was to be permanently excluded from kinship by order of none other than Moses himself. In the book of Ruth however, the principal family find in that foreign place of exile what was lacking back home.

In biblical narratives it is often the case that those who leave to find food return home as changed people. This was undoubtedly true of Abram in Genesis 12 and 13 when he fled to Egypt during a famine and returned home a wealthy man and able to secure his foothold in the Promised Land. The same happens to the sons of Jacob, who return by way of the exodus as a nation large enough to take possession of the land their ancestors had left.

On the surface it seems that Naomi's story is an exception. She, with Elimelech, is displaced by famine into Moab and returns, in her own mind at least, manifestly reduced. The women of the town who greet her are astonished and barely recognize her as the woman who left all those years ago, while Naomi herself draws attention to her tragic self-perception (Ruth 1.19–21). As the story unfolds, however, it reveals something different: that the kindness of her daughter-in-law is worth more than all riches or numerical advantage. One of the real surprises of the story is that the people of Bethlehem are enriched not by plundering their enemies but by finding space to welcome the stranger into their midst and to be changed – in practice and policy – by that stranger. In this way the traditional trope of flight from famine and being enriched in the strange place is radically renewed. The foreigner, who has options to remain at home, instead, because of her generosity, enriches the community that had once been impoverished by a famine of food and morality. This in its turn draws radical acts of generosity in response from the people.

Ruth's kindnesses are not simply the niceness of polite company. Three times in this short story Ruth puts her life at risk. In chapter 1, she is determined to leave her homeland to accompany Naomi back to Bethlehem. In chapter 2, she risks assault by gleaning in the fields during harvest (Boaz repeatedly warns his employees to leave her alone). And in chapter 3, she puts life and reputation at risk to lie with Boaz on the threshing-room floor. This is no ordinary goodness but the kind that is willing to take personal risk to look out for the welfare of another, and what the story exposes is that each account of risk-taking kindness is motivated by her relationship with Naomi.

Ruth consistently takes the emptinesses of the story and transforms them into plenty, and in so doing she draws similar acts of kindness and generosity from those around her. Take Naomi, for instance: initially silenced by grief and trauma, she nevertheless allows Ruth to accompany her back to Bethlehem even if it is possibly done with a degree of sullenness. There is no conversation recorded between them on their journey back to Naomi's hometown. And when they get to the gates of the town and are met by the women, who are staggered by how depleted Naomi is, she complains that though she went away with plenty she has returned with nothing (1.21). How must this lament have been heard by Ruth, who is presumably standing within earshot? The chapter continues with the silence of Naomi, but who hasn't known those times of distress and sorrow when no words are possible? Ruth meets that incapacity with words designed to address the need and takes it on herself to risk the fields.

Naomi never fully loses herself in grief though: she still refers to Ruth as 'daughter' in Ruth 2.2, and by the end of the chapter she appears to be returning to some measure of capacity. The happy coincidence of Ruth's landing in Boaz's fields draws from her an expression of delight and even hope that their circumstances could now be transformed (2.20).

The silent Naomi of chapter 2 is gone by the beginning of chapter 3, and now she responds with determination in seeking to secure a future for Ruth (though it must be acknowledged it is Ruth who takes all the risks). Once again relational language is prominent in the chapter, as Naomi refers again and again to this foreigner as 'daughter' (3.1, 16, 18). This is in sharp contrast to the opening two chapters of the story, where Ruth is almost never mentioned without reference to her ethnicity by other characters in the story and even by the narrator. While there is a solidarity among the widowed women in the story, including Orpah, this is in contrast to the attitudes of the men like Boaz's manager, who refers to Ruth as the Moabite from Moab (2.6).

Boaz is undoubtedly a man of some stature in the community; he owns fields, he employs workers and he has the capacity to summon the elders of the town to hear his legal case, as narrated in chapter 4. He also seems to be respected by his employees, even blessing them as he arrives in the workplace (2.4), a blessing they return. He also resists the ethnic stereotyping of those around him by referring to Ruth as 'daughter' repeatedly in both chapters 2 and 3. This is a kindness that almost overwhelms Ruth in 2.10, causing her to bow to the ground in thanks. The surprise to her is that Boaz has noticed her, a foreigner (2.10), which may be an indication of how invisible she otherwise was in that community. Behind this comment of Ruth's lies a whole world of pain, and we would be rightfully astonished that despite her precarious status she has persisted in her love and concern for Naomi. The fact that Boaz is aware of her story in 2.11–12 is also an indication that however studied the attempts were by others to render her invisible, her goodness had a way of penetrating even the hardest of hearts.

What is curious about Boaz is that, good and kind as he is, he fails to follow through on his responsibilities to Ruth and Naomi, despite his obvious physical attraction to Ruth. He doesn't match his recognition of her kindness with corresponding action. This forces Ruth to go to even more dangerous lengths to get this man to do what he was required to do under the Law. The narrative tension in chapter 3 is whether or not Boaz's kindness towards her will translate into treating her as kin. It is one thing to be generous towards strangers, it is quite another to subvert the prejudices of the town and accept this woman as family. So when he addresses her twice as 'daughter' in 3.10–11 and refers to her kindness and good character, the tension is relieved, but not fully.

And it is here that we come to the truly radical heart of the story. While it is one thing to respond with compassion to need as it presents itself on the doorstep, it is quite another to address the circumstances that caused the need in the first place. I liken this to the difference between compassionate action – seen in something like the proliferation of food banks run by churches to address food poverty – and civic advocacy for policy change to relieve the causes of poverty, which happens when churches coordinate their activity, share their statistics on need, and lobby government to change its economic and social policies. Both are needed, but one without the other is limited in its capacity to change society. Ruth chapter 3 is the compassionate action; chapter 4 is the advocacy for policy change.

When Boaz agrees at this point to do the right thing

(finally), by placing his personal acceptance of Ruth as kin before the people of the town for their endorsement or otherwise, it is an extraordinary act of kindness and goodness that also involves him in considerable risk. Would the people follow through on their knowledge of Ruth as a woman of good character, or would the power of history and tradition rest too heavily on their shoulders? Boaz seems confident that, if this is done in the appropriate way, the people will shed years of prejudice against Moabites and welcome Ruth into kinship.

And so Boaz gathers the elders of the town to witness a formal, legal arrangement between himself and the other relative with a claim on Naomi's land (4.1–2). It also seems that quite a crowd has gathered (4.4, 9, 11). And just so no one can be in any doubt as to what is about to transpire, Boaz returns to Ruth's ethnic origin by referring to her as Ruth the Moabite (4.5) – we haven't encountered that language in the story in quite a while. What follows seems bizarre to us, but it was an ancient method of sealing legal arrangements.

There are many legal practices in the book of Ruth, some of which are directed towards the social protection of vulnerable people, such as when Ruth goes into the fields to glean in chapter 2. But this practice in chapter 4, when this unnamed relative of Boaz and Naomi takes off his sandal to effectively seal the deal to buy land, might seem strange to us. Just what on earth is being achieved here and why preserve this tiny detail? As with so much in this apparently simple book, there is a huge transformation being covered by this tiny detail that has significance not just for Ruth but also for many of the contemporary challenges people of faith face in our rapidly changing world. The implications of this tradition also have significance for how we read the entire Bible and make sense of it in our time. But you would hardly know it from the surface. It is the outcome of this bizarre tradition that may make Ruth the most radical book in the whole of the Scriptures.

When this anonymous relative removes his sandal he is following the instructions of the Law in Deuteronomy 25.7–10, and at the same time acquiring a reputation for himself and his family as the kind of people who don't follow through on their obligations:

> But if the man has no desire to marry his brother's widow, then his brother's widow shall go up to the elders at the gate and say, 'My husband's brother refuses to perpetuate his brother's name in Israel; he will not perform the duty of a husband's brother to me.' Then the elders of his town shall summon him and speak to him. If he persists, saying, 'I have no desire to marry her', then his brother's wife shall go up to him in the presence of the elders, pull his sandal off his foot, spit in his face, and declare, 'This is what is done to the man who does not build up his brother's house.' Throughout Israel his family shall be known as 'the house of him whose sandal was pulled off.'

Significantly, this law in Deuteronomy is about preserving family lines. This reluctant relative has done some shrewd calculations and we can imagine what they might be. Initially he thinks that he can buy the land and thereby extend his wealth (Ruth 4.4). But when he subsequently learns that he must also marry Ruth the Moabite – this is where the reminder of Ruth's ethnicity is so important – to preserve the family line of Elimelech, he immediately withdraws from the deal. Perhaps he calculates that since Ruth is still capable of bearing children, any child he has with Ruth will inherit some, if not all, of his estate. But since he regards her as the

Moabite, this will mean the land passing out of family own-ership, and thus his family's share in the blessing of God in the land will leave Israel entirely. Marrying Ruth only makes sense for him if he considers her as kin. He doesn't, and so the deal is off. By acting this way, the unnamed relative – and it is surely significant that he is unnamed – is actually holding firmly to a certain interpretation of the Law of Moses that permanently prohibits the admittance of Moabites into the people of God (Deut. 23.3).

Now Boaz reveals his full intention, and he calls all the people and the elders to witness what he is doing (Ruth 4.9). He intends to marry Ruth and have children with her, and he will treat their children as having full inheritance rights in Israel. And, again, he reminds them that they are witnesses (4.10). And everyone enthusiastically agrees.

We shouldn't move too quickly past this moment, for what is happening here is remarkable. Boaz has placed before the people a clear moment of transformation, and they have accepted it. The choice they faced was to hold tightly to the tradition of Moses laid out in the Law in Deuteronomy and refuse to admit Ruth to the community. The Law is clear and unequivocal on this matter. But in this time and in these circumstances and for this woman, the application of the Law would have resulted in an unkindness or un-grace. Knowing her character and kindness, the people agreed that this particular Law had come to the end of its useful life. And so they take to themselves the right, and even, I would argue, the obligation, to change the Law and the tradition so that kindness and grace is extended.

Pause here for a moment.

In this apparently simple story we are presented with an extraordinary example of how the Bible works. This seems to me to be an example of the Bible reinterpreting itself and

76

its tradition for new circumstances. There was a time, perhaps, when the existence of a good Moabite was impossible to imagine. But times change, and with that the application of the Law. There was a time when belonging could only be determined by blood: those considered as kin were people who looked exactly like us, and spoke and behaved exactly like us. But times change, and with that the application of the Law. And those changes are always in the direction of kindness and grace.

We will always wrestle with the temptation to define belonging through an application of law that is unbending. But if the application of the law results in unkindness, however unintended or regretted, then this should be considered bad law and should be altered. Even if it is the Law of Moses. Or the canon law, or the word of the ecclesiastical courts, or the various codes, or the books of concord or practice, however our ecclesial communities define their rules.

The chain reaction of *chesed*

The story of Ruth is a story of kindness. In fact it is a story of multiple kindnesses that cascade one after the other until they overflow in a change in the whole tradition of a people to extend kindness to a stranger. The chain reaction begins with Naomi's prayer that God would deal *chesed* to Orpah and Ruth in Ruth 1.8, and tumbles on through Ruth's abiding loyalty to Naomi, Boaz's kindness in protecting Ruth, and on and on until a whole community is moved to make room for this remarkable woman. And it challenges us today about how our laws and practices as peoples deal similar kindness to those who are vulnerable or strangers among us. It challenges us on how we speak kindly and with grace towards those who voted in a different way from us in the referendum, or think differently from us on the issue of the border.

It challenges us on who we consider kin and how an outsider becomes one of us. It dares us to imagine the domino effect of a single act of grace. It calls us to greater levels of empathy towards those who struggle day to day to survive among us, to feed their family, access health care, find some purpose in their lives. Like butterfly wings in the Amazon changing weather patterns around our two islands, we are called not to great acts of national upheaval but to do the great work of kindness and grace with those around us, and to believe that these could have unimaginable impact at the national level in our neighbouring countries. To ignore the political importance of kindness or to dismiss it as insubstantial or peripheral in our current difficulties is to open the door to all manner of malign forces and to contribute to the rot in our civic discourse. Without the presence of grace and kindness we risk the public square being overrun by conflict.

In his recent book *On the Brink of Everything: Grace, Gravity, and Getting Old*, the American sociologist and contemplative Parker J. Palmer wrote, 'Violence is what happens when we don't know what else to do with our suffering.'[1]

This has made me think over recent days. Is the violence of our division here in Ireland, the killing and maiming violence; the verbal and even physical violence of Brexit; the violence of how we care and don't care – is it all an attempt to make some meaning and purpose out of the meaninglessness of our suffering?

Christianity responds to the dilemma of what to do with our suffering, of what to do with our violence and division,

---

1 Oakland, CA: Berrett-Koehler Publishers, 2018, p. 160.

with acts of lovingkindness. This is our big idea. Kindness. Kindness and grace overcome violence and division. Kindness can transcend division, sometimes by taking into itself the suffering.

This is our big idea.

Kindness is more than just do-goodery, which has some value of course, in that it can help relieve suffering. But it can also be about the salving of our own conscience.

Kindness is never naive about how the world is. It is a choice to love in the face of division.

Kindness is courage lived out. Maya Angelou said, 'Have enough courage to trust love one more time and always one more time.'

Kindness subverts traditional divisions by bringing in those who everyone else seeks to keep out, and reaches out to those who others wish to keep at arms' length.

Kindness is never constrained by the rules. Kindness changes the rules. And laws.

Kindness acts for the benefit of others and never for ourselves or our institutions and organizations.

Kindness sees beyond divisions of ethnicity or politics or religion and finds the common good through service.

8

The Fourth Act of the Book of Ruth

PÁDRAIG Ó TUAMA

Israel is regenerated by the woman from Moab.[1]

Does a word carry power in its proclamation, or is the power of a word assigned? J. K. Rowling's Harry Potter series circles around this, with word-spells like 'Avada kedavra' carrying the power to kill, although notably the person using this curse must wish it to work, as well as proclaim it. Much literature – religious and not – concerns itself with the question of what a name means. Linguists, too, debate whether a word carries a meaning unique to itself or whether humans have innate senses of meaning that seek expression through language. All of this is made even more complex when the question of a person's name is considered.

'Not in my name' we read in signs and objections around the world. Shakespeare was concerned with names. When Juliet Capulet fell in love with Romeo Montague they were immediately plunged into the drama – and tragedy – of names. The Capulets and Montagues were sworn enemies. To be with someone from the other house was to bring a

---

1 Avivah Zornberg, *The Murmuring Deep* (New York: Schocken Books, 2009), p. 368.

blight upon your own. Juliet muses on the nature of names, at once recognizing that a name is just a sound we make to attach meaning to something, but also that a name holds power. 'O be some other name!' she says.

> 'Tis but thy name that is my enemy.
> Thou art thyself, though not a Montague.
> What's Montague? It is nor hand nor foot,
> Nor arm nor face, nor any other part
> Belonging to a man. O be some other name.
> What's in a name? That which we call a rose
> By any other word would smell as sweet.
> So Romeo would, were he not Romeo called.[2]

Names of sworn enemies are one thing; muddying a name is another. 'Your name is mud' we say in English, perhaps playing both on the idea of useless dirt and Dr Samuel Mudd, a man imprisoned for his part in conspiring to execute Abraham Lincoln. 'My name is tarnished', some people say, using a word that probably comes from Old French words meaning dim, conceal, hide. There is a belief in this word that there is something shiny that can be covered by something else: shame, perhaps, or a slur. People go to all kinds of lengths to rescue their reputation, and to all kinds of lengths to tarnish that of another. Reputation is a cultural phenomenon: what gives a person repute in one era is different from that of another. For some, being childless is a tarnished reputation – the imagination being that their circumstances are a punishment for some wrongdoing. For others, reneging on a legal duty is a damaging of reputation. For still others, falling on hard times is a damaging of reputation, the imagination being that the downfall was some kind of karma: deserved

---

2 William Shakespeare, *Romeo and Juliet* (London: Heinemann, 2010), Act 2, Scene 2.

for some known or unknown reason. Reputation is primal in us: just look at what we'll do to win.

When it comes to the question of names and reputations, there are perhaps three concerns to think of: survival, reputation and legacy. These concerns range from the immediate – Will I survive the tarnishing of my name? – to the public – What will people think of me? – to the future – How will I be remembered? I met a man once whose work involved incentivizing despotic business leaders to bring their companies into greater accountability. He assured them of a guaranteed income, and then spoke of both reputation and legacy. He played, in other words, both to pride and pragmatics.

Pride and pragmatics play a part in the question of names in the book of Ruth too: Naomi – or as she has called herself now, Mara – is concerned with the dignity of her reputation in providing for Ruth, her Moabite daughter-in-law. Ruth, most commonly called Ruth the Moabite, is known by her origins, rarely her actions; Elimelech, Naomi's dead husband, has a name that implies he wishes to be great without acting accordingly; and Boaz's name could mean swiftness, strength or sharp mind.

In the fourth and final act of this drama, Ruth and Naomi are offstage and Boaz seeks a legal hearing with the kinsman who, technically, has a greater 'claim' on Ruth. Levirate marriage declares that a woman left childless after the death of her husband will be married by a brother – or other male relative – of the dead man, who will give her children; children who will carry the name of the dead husband. So if Ruth had been an Israelite, any child she had with a future husband would have been known as the children of Mahlon. This honours the name of the dead husband, provides an income and reputation for the widow, and – it is supposed – ties them all in a line of legacy. However, two difficulties are in the way of Ruth: first, the recognition of her marriage is debatable because of being from Moab; and second, even if her marriage is to be recognized, there's a closer cousin of her dead husband than Boaz.

Ruth's story embodies a story of change: will the people she's chosen decide to recognize her marriage and accept where her desires lie? These are both personal and legal matters. The relationship between Israelite and Moabite territory is narrowed into a singular story of a particular woman. It seems that Ruth's marriage will be recognized because of her devotion (or to give it the correct term, *chesed*: loving-kindness) to her mother-in-law. This is beneficial for her but perhaps problematic for policy. What if Ruth hadn't demonstrated any lovingkindness out of the ordinary – wouldn't she still have been entitled to legal and welfare recognition and provision? In any event, the circumstance of her nationality means that her kindness is an affront and even a challenge to the stereotypes by which her people were caricatured. Due to determination and risk, and the subsequent recognition by Boaz, it seems her widowhood is recognized, and she has been allowed to glean in a field, unassaulted, like anybody else in her circumstances should have been entitled to, without having to be so brave.

The legal question of a subsequent marriage now arises. Who is 'entitled' to consider her as marriage partner? Who is she obliged to consider, and in what order? That she and Boaz have an attachment has been clear since the second chapter. However, there is a male cousin whose 'claim' is stronger because of being of nearer kin than Boaz. This closer cousin is, according to the Midrash, known by the unfortunate name of Peloni Almoni; that is, So-and-So. In the scheme of the drama he is caricatured as a foil, a fool perhaps, and his role is pivotal but unidimensional.

In many countries there are names like 'So-and-So'. In Ireland we might say 'Whatshisface' or 'Yerman' or 'Yermano'. In some contexts we might say 'Himself', or even 'Horse'. These substitutes for names can come across as endearments, humour or sectarianism. They can indicate a setting up of an everyman type character whose anonymity is meant to be the blank canvas on whom stereotypes can be pinned, or they can represent the anonymizing of a person whose identity and importance are being denied. A character like So-and-So is often important in the unfolding of a particularly good anecdote, and our practice of this type of storytelling in Ireland is not unique; we see it here in the book of Ruth too: a man whose name is such that the narrator doesn't see him as important, but who represents a foil in the development of the plot. In some stories the So-and-So character becomes the hero or does something so noteworthy that readers begin to speculate about the identity of the character. Not here.

Names open up the door to characters: Naomi seeks to re-establish her name by providing a good husband for her daughter-in-law. Boaz's name is being demonstrated by his actions. So-and-So, Elimelech, Mahlon and Chilion are – controversially and significantly – being slowly erased both from the narrative and from the genealogy. Ruth's child will eventually be named as the son of Boaz, not the son of Mahlon – and all of these changes are coming about due to their association with a Moabite from Moab named Ruth. She acts according to her own self at every point, and in her integrity is found courage, fortitude and lovingkindness. She is a turning point for law, and law turns towards her with the same love with which she supported Naomi. I read once, in a Kabbalistic text that I've since forgotten the name of, that Torah is one of the names for God. Law turned towards Ruth. God turned towards Ruth.

The ending of this extraordinary book links Ruth in a long line of ancestors building towards a legacy that will be furthered by King David. In the genealogy of this text there are ten generations from Perez to David, Ruth being David's great-grandmother. She is not the only foreigner included in the line: Tamar is the mother of Perez and she, too, has a notable story. Ruth and Tamar are bound up in stories of public comment upon childlessness, dead husbands and self-reliance. Tamar had two dead husbands and was refused the right of marriage of the third brother by Judah, the older brother of Joseph (see Genesis 38). Both Ruth and Tamar are subject to the whims of men in their observance of law, and both of them are praised for their actions, even though readers might wish that they had simply been accorded what they were entitled to because they were entitled to it, not because they'd demonstrated they were 'worthy' of it. Ruth and Tamar, Moabite and Canaanite, are two foreign women wrapped into the story of redemption that seeks its culmination in the life of David. They show that belonging is thicker than blood.

The story of Ireland, and our relationship with Britain, has a long history. Probably 700 years, maybe 800. It's longer, too, with the patron saint of Ireland being a Latin-speaking man kidnapped from Britain and trafficked to Ireland. To speak of purity and enmity in the context of Ireland and Britain is to be selective on a narrative retelling of the past. The past is not so convenient as to render idealism inscrutable. The book of Ruth compels its readers to examine their story of the past, to recognize that so-called fellow citizens – often so-called simply because of an accident of birth – can be far less trustworthy than those whose actions are valorous but whose identity is suspect likewise simply because of an accident of birth.

Boaz is shown in a particular light in this fourth chapter. Where he is initially depicted as open-hearted, devoted and considerate towards Ruth, he is now depicted as shrewd, knowledgeable and perhaps even mildly manipulative in his dealings with So-and-So. Boaz calls a gathering by going to the gate of the town. So-and-So passes by and Boaz invites him over with, 'Come over, friend; sit down here.'

How did Boaz know that this passing-by would be so convenient? What is the friend about? Is this strictly friendly? Boaz gathers ten other men as witnesses and proceeds to present his case – with his own particular spin. First he speaks of Naomi returning from Moab and her desire now to sell the parcel of land. (It is notable that Naomi would not have inherited this land because of the death of her own husband, but because of the deaths of her sons.) Boaz presents the story simply, in such a way that So-and-So's desire to assert his first claim to the land would come easily. You have first claim to it, and I have second, Boaz says. 'I will redeem it', So-and-So says. So far so satisfactory, for So-and-So. And for Boaz, but So-and-So doesn't know that yet.

Now Boaz's scheming comes into play. He speaks of the requirement of the redeemer of this land of Naomi's to acquire the Moabite. Perhaps nowhere else in the book is 'Moabite' used more powerfully. Boaz seems to be playing on the prejudice of So-and-So. He doesn't only mention Ruth's nationality, he lays out the obligation of the law: 'The day you acquire the field from the hand of Naomi, you are also acquiring Ruth the Moabite, the widow of the dead man, to maintain the dead man's name on his inheritance' (4.5). It seems unlikely that So-and-So is ignorant of the reasons for, or responsibilities of, Levirate law. Boaz seems to be making sure to push So-and-So – in public – to acknowledge what his obligations towards Ruth would be were he to marry her. He seems to guess – or perhaps know – the prejudices of So-and-So towards Moabites, and he creates a situation where exposure and expediency are part of the negotiation. Perhaps Boaz's name means Swiftness after all. He is portrayed as a compelling man too. He has land, he issues orders and men obey. He sits and calls, and men gather. Ruth and Boaz are being depicted as two individuals – separated by law, land, religion and protocol – whose public actions are marked by determination.

In any case, Boaz's speculation was correct. So-and-So does not wish to damage his 'inheritance'. This innocuous word is important here. So-and-So clearly owns land already, so he is not waiting on an inheritance for himself. By damaging an inheritance, he seems to be talking about the future. The inheritance that he would pass on to his own sons would be spoiled by marrying a Moabite in the present. In the name of preventing something in the future that he finds distasteful, he is sacrificing a gain in the present. He is acting both unwisely and unkindly. But that's the plan: Boaz's rhetoric and staging has helped the imagined to become realized, publicly, in the presence of witnesses. Boaz is using So-and-So's lack of kindness against him.

Why would So-and-So turn down the possibility of acquiring land? Perhaps he fears he'd go the same way as Mahlon, and die. Or he worries about the impact of a future son of his being designated as the son of Mahlon. In Ruth Rabbah, Rabbi Samuel the son of Nachman takes this further: he guesses that So-and-So did not know the words of Torah. Speaking in the imagined voice of So-and-So, Rabbi Samuel the son of Nachman said: 'The first ones did not die but rather because they took her and I am going to go and take her? I certainly am not going to take her. I will not pollute my seed and I am not going to create unfitness for my children' (Ruth

Rabbah, chapter 7). Strong words – speaking of Naomi's sons' deaths as punishment for marrying a Moabite, and speaking of pollution by association. This brings us back once again to the question of reputation and legacy. In the name of both reputation and legacy, So-and-So is willing to sacrifice the thing that would have provided more survivability to him and his family. He seems willing to be poorer in order to be purer. Expediency does not guide many decisions: imaginations about purity, identity, reputation and legacy seem to be more powerful in the mind than land is underfoot. To So-and-So, association with Ruth the Moabite seems to be akin to death.

So-and-So is a foil, a caricature, a trope, but also serves as a warning. My guess is that we are not so much called to identify and expel the So-and-So character in our midst as to find the So-and-So within ourselves, to recognize how fear of taint can corrupt our capacity to do business, to demonstrate kindness, and to act according to deep ideals of hospitality and the loving foundations of law.

Boaz declares his intention towards Ruth, and the witnesses reply with:

> We are witnesses. May the LORD make the woman who is coming into your house like Rachel and Leah, who together built up the house of Israel. May you produce children in Ephrathah and bestow a name in Bethlehem; and, through the children that the LORD will give you by this young woman, may your house be like the house of Perez, whom Tamar bore to Judah. (Ruth 4.11–12)

Here, the crowd of witnesses speak as one – they bless Ruth, drawing on the deep legacy of other foreign women who are heroes and matriarchs of Israel: Rachel, Leah and Tamar.

They fold Ruth into a story of pride, legacy and inheritance and, indeed, a name. She is given foremothers, and the family of Ruth and Boaz is also given a narrative inheritance. The crowd of men function like a subsidiary chorus to the crowd of women who've already been introduced at the return of Naomi. Now, when Ruth gives birth to a son, the women say:

> Blessed be the LORD, who has not left you this day without next-of-kin; and may his name be renowned in Israel! He shall be to you a restorer of life and a nourisher of your old age; for your daughter-in-law who loves you, who is more to you than seven sons, has borne him. (4.14–15)

One way of understanding these chorus voices is theatrical: dramatists have used chorus voices for millennia to give a reprieve, for humour and hyperbole, or to reinforce the storyline for any of the audience who were distracted. However, the function of the chorus in the book of Ruth also highlights the communal nature of individual acts of courage. At no point are the chorus voices chiming in to commit – in advance – support and inclusion for a possible action. The voices only chime in with their support once a courageous person has taken lonely and virtuous action. To act with virtue in the face of prejudice is often isolating, and only when others have little to fear will they voice their support for the very courageous actions they had previously either decried or – at best – denied.

In the end, another law is changed as a result of Ruth the Moabite coming to Israel from Moab. Her kindness was a political force, her particularity changed the way a people considered border-crossers, inter-cultural marriages and provisions, and her association with Boaz meant that she was written into the David storyline, and Boaz – not her dead husband – is named as the father. Laws and names and legacy and families are redefined by lovingkindness. Blood may spill, but love lasts forever.

Now these are the descendants of Perez: Perez became the father of Hezron, Hezron of Ram, Ram of Amminadab, Amminadab of Nahshon, Nahshon of Salmon, Salmon of Boaz, Boaz of Obed, Obed of Jesse, and Jesse of David. (4.18–21)

9

Afterword

PÁDRAIG Ó TUAMA

I am writing this in a time of pandemic. Covid-19 has shut down industries, art houses, places of worship, places of work. People's jobs have been cut, exam results have been estimated and re-estimated, and the announcements of the numbers of infections and deaths continue. Low today. Rising tomorrow. Not as bad as last month. Worse than six months ago. The start of the end of this plague. The end of the start of this virus. Glenn died about a week after George Floyd was murdered in Minneapolis in the United States. We'd talked on the phone about George Floyd, and Glenn was talking about the need for projects where white Irish people explore our whiteness – we who have often used the suffering we've endured to imagine that we couldn't impose suffering on others are in need of imagining ourselves through some of the racial realities we'd rather ignore than acknowledge.

This was the like of him – to see what was happening in the world and imagine that he was part of the problem and that therefore serious conversion was needed.

In editing this book I've been reminded again and again of how Glenn defined the function of theology: to be at the hinge-point of conversion, always ready to learn, always ready to change, always ready to watch with wonder at what justice looks like in public; to imagine that something that might be something like God is present in the events that are demanding justice, change, deep respect and kindness.

Glenn was far more comfortable than I in the north. He'd phone sometimes to wind me up, telling me a story of some Tory politician who'd said something derogatory about Ireland, or the Irish language being leprechaun-sounding. He thought this was hilarious, and he'd laugh as I swore. I'm all fire. He was as patient as the dawn.

This book is, in many senses, a meditation on time and pain. How, in the centuries of British presence in Ireland, do we make sense of British and Irish stories in Ireland now, where so many people – of all national and religious identities – have suffered? Each side has its own griefs and grievances. Your people killed my lover. Your people took my language. Your people killed indiscriminately. Your people didn't use peaceful means to achieve political ends. Your people endorsed robbery by calling it a national project. Your people murdered. Your people murdered. Your people started it. Your people started it. You're to blame. No, you are.

Griefs cross boundaries. Families in England are marked by the griefs of murders of sons and daughters who died in Belfast serving in the British armies. Families in Ireland are marked by similar griefs in the opposite directions. Interrelatedness is a fact of blood and history in Ireland and Britain. Disparate particularities, yes – many of them in each identity – but interrelatedness all the same. Grief is not a game. It might be possible to say your grief will be my grief, your people, my people.

It is almost the end of 2020. In late spring 2021 a centenary will be marked. The centenary of the partition of Ireland, some will call it. The centenary of the formation of Northern Ireland, others will call it. Some will celebrate, some will lament. Ultimately – and this is a strange union – many people in Ireland will be united by bewilderment at how little English people know about English involvement in Ireland. We are used to hearing voices on English radio speaking about 'you over there' as if we over here decided to partition ourselves all on our own. So is the solution a united annoyance against our nearest neighbours? That won't save us either.

We began a practice during the Brexit and Ruth engagements: telling and evoking stories of honour where often there are stories of accusation. This wasn't a diversionary practice. It was a radical practice. The public debates about Brexit and EU membership had ramped up negative nationalisms that imagined solitary identities: I am English and only English; I am Irish and only Irish. I am ... you get it. But there are many families in Britain or Ireland that have relied – for love or money, or many other things – on support from another jurisdiction. Therefore, in a media frenzy that amplified stories designed for clickbait and annoyance, we asked rooms of people to amplify other stories amid the fray – stories of gratitude, of generosity, of dependency – and asked how it would be if our public discussions were framed with such an ethic. This was not *Won't-it-all-be-nice-if-we-have-a-cup-of-tea-together?* This was the practice of generosity in the face of manipulation; this is the stuff that hope is built on. This is the stuff – my God! – that we hope to God our public voices could practise, instead of dismantling some of the very structures that have begun a fragile peace for the peoples of Ireland and Britain. To be yoked to each other is a fact: but we can do more than tolerate being yoked together. We can flourish – this requires courage, and conviction and kindness and critique and plain speaking, both about gratitudes and griefs. This only comes with practice, with the courageous and steady work of extending gratitude and respect even in terse times. If we can't speak kindness to each other, critique won't be received either. And we need both, in these times in these islands of Britain and Ireland: kindness and critique. Each must serve the other.

The orbits of our own Irish and British griefs with and around each other need to be held within a storytelling framework that is confident about something: we will kill each other unless we can turn to each other. Brexit is coming. So is the centenary of whatever we call it, depending on how-ever we see it. Glenn's chapter on Compassion and the Law is, I think, the most important one in this book. For him, faithfulness is demonstrated – not derogated – in the capacity to change, in the capacity to share, in the capacity to make law serve an ethic of interconnectedness, and to let policy and practice follow on that ethic, rather than sacrifice ethics to a law that is made immovable, and therefore as brutal as it is brittle. This, for him, was the mandate of his public theology: to change towards the lovingkindness that will change us. This is as much required in the work of loving your friends as it is in the work of loving people on different sides of a political divide.

Glenn and I were moved by the sponsorship of the Fund for Reconciliation from the Government of Ireland. And by the sponsorship of the Community Relations Council in North-ern Ireland, as well as the Henry Luce Foundation in the United States. Politicians and senior civil servants with Irish, British and EU responsibilities lent this project support and space. Our colleagues in Corrymeela were – and continue to be – a generous and creative and supportive community who believe that something called *together* might help us trans-form a society where we share land into a society where we share more than land. We met thousands of people – across

Britain and Ireland – over the course of the planning of this book. Their thoughts shaped and challenged and changed us. Glenn's yellow notebooks are filled with quotes from individuals who showed that the bloodlines of Britain and Ireland run deep through all families. It is our deep honour that this book was published by Canterbury Press, under the careful curation of Christine Smith.

The last word is a word of love. For all his public theology, Glenn's first love was family. They grieve the loss of public life, but far more the loss of his private life, the life that revolved around them, his centres, the joys of his heart, the *grá* at the heart of all things. It is to them – Adrienne, Philippa and Christopher – that this book owes its deepest gratitude.

Discussion Questions and Prayers

Discussion: Chapter 1

1 Can you think of an occasion in your own life when real-life encounter with someone considered as 'other' changed your opinion of them in a positive direction? What elements in the encounter brought about the change?
2 Given the enormity of the challenges facing the world, in what ways have you found yourself tempted to disengage from what is happening?
3 In what ways have liturgy and the regular practices of your faith helped keep your gaze focused on the suffering of the world?
4 In what ways have recent crises we've faced turned our attention towards mutual self-reliance? Kindness towards the other? Selfishness?

Prayer

God of bodies,
if it is true that the earth is yours
and all within it,
then yours are the rocks and grasses
on every side
of every border.

And – more –
yours are the faces
of every person:
border-dwellers, border-crossers,
border-guards, border-deniers,
border-defenders, borderless,
borderful, border-endangered
and border-dreamers.
What we ask is simple,
but it will take many lifetimes:
let us make borders serve us,
not us them.
And – again – let us
be people who make justice
stretch across borders.
Because the earth is yours
and everything in it.
It is round
and everything turns on itself.
May we turn to each other
as we turn to you.
Amen.

Discussion: Chapter 2

1 If 'a hunger for leadership' is part of the story of Ruth, what leadership forms are on display in chapter 1?

2 How would you characterize the leadership offered by politicians, business, civic or community leaders in our recent crises?

3 In the spaces created between our different opinions, attitudes or beliefs, what kinds of dialogue might be possible?

4 How can we build the courage to step across bordered
   differences?

Prayer

We say we hunger for leaders
but it is difficult to know who to vote for.

We say we deny some of our leaders
but they keep getting elected.

We know that votes split a people
and we ache to raise our voice.

We celebrate when a young leader rises up
and we wait for them to fall.

We look to the tried and trusted leaders
and remember their many failures.

We hope our leaders will fulfil promises
and we struggle when they compromise.

We elect some leaders
and other leaders seem to rise up from the earth.

We want our leaders to tell us what we need to hear
and we struggle when they tell us what we need to hear.

We hold our leaders responsible
and we query the models of leadership we support.

We wish our leaders safety and health
so they can deepen our safety and health.

We wish our leaders intelligence and information
and a sound mind and a steady heart.

We do not wish to have the leaders we deserve
but the leaders we need.

We have made our leaders saviours
and have forced these saviours on others.

We speak about leaders
as if we were not all leaders.

We think our leaders need to look like us
but our leaders do not need to look like us.

We are many different kinds
and we need many different things.

We want leaders to lead us into the future
and we know that leaders often need to point to the past.

We are people in the present
hoping that courage can guide us to a safer future.

Discussion: Chapter 3

1 Where in the book of Ruth do you see people acting out national stereotypes?
2 What stories do you tell about the neighbouring town, city or nation? What stories do they tell about you? Examine those stories for what they might say about both of you.
3 What raw material might exist for the construction of a new story of relationship with your neighbouring town, city or nation?
4 Tell a story of someone in your experience who defied the stereotypes.

Prayer

When I was a child I thought like a child.
My country good; theirs evil.
Or: my country is bad; theirs is better;
Or: my country is poor; my country is corrupt;
Or: my country is recovering from empire.
When I was a child,
I thought the stories I told
were the stories every country told.

Now,
looking at maps, and borders,
new lines on old land,
and remembering stories of people
who crossed rivers and oceans,
seeing the twists of my family's history,
knowing that the DNA that twists in me
is more legion than the stories I've inherited,

I turn to the story of my country
and make it
be many.

Discussion: Chapter 4

1 Ruth, Naomi and Orpah's decisions are ones that most will never understand, and imaginations of what it was like will always fail. How can acknowledging that many of us will never face what they faced help us in taking their circumstances seriously?

2 Reflect for a moment on an occasion when you were the first to do something. What emotions were discernible in you? What struggles and freedoms? What did the experience leave behind in you?

3 In this part of the story the reader is struck both by Boaz's capacity to see Ruth (2.5) and Ruth's surprise, relief or joy at being noticed, and not in a predatory way (2.10). Take a moment to review your day. Is there anyone you failed to notice at the time?

4 Ruth's surprise is related to being recognized for more than her foreignness. How can we ensure that our recognition of neighbours consists of noting more than their difference from us?

Prayer

We watch as Ruth says, 'Where you go, I'll go.'
And we watch as Orpah decides to return, knowing that she'd rather be with her family than burden Naomi.
And we watch Naomi, a husk of herself, go back to where she came from,

wondering what her welcome will be like.
And we do not understand.
Help us, as we do not understand, to watch, listen,
believe, and trust, that the things people do
in desperation are – usually – the best they can imagine
    to do.
And move us from judgement into belief:
belief of these three women making choices
they never thought they'd have to make.
Help us keep distance, not imagining that we would
    do better
in circumstances like these.
Because how would we know?
May we watch. May we honour. May we believe.
May we support where support is asked for.
May we learn where learning is needed.

Discussion: Chapter 5

1   In what ways, if at all, has weariness of the news affected
    you in recent years? How have you dealt with it?
2   In the course of national debates or crises, to what extent
    do you think fear has been a driver for protagonists on all
    sides? How has this been expressed?
3   How can we make appropriate space to hear quieter
    stories or counter-narratives?

Prayer

The Lord be with you
And also with you.

The Lord be with those in joy
and also with those in sorrow.

The Lord be with those waiting for news
and also with those avoiding the news.

The Lord be with those drowning in scandal
and also with those scanning headlines for scandal.

The Lord be with them
because the Lord is with us.

The Lord be in our tired bones
and in our rising too.

The Lord is a steady help in times of need
and times of need are all around us.

The Lord grant us a quiet night
so that we can love those whose nights are not.

The Lord grant us a wakeful morning
where rest can help us listen.

The Lord be with us
and with everyone we love.

The Lord be with us
and with everyone we don't.

The Lord grant us enough space
to hear what's calling for our attention.

Discussion: Chapter 6

1 Does it matter or not to you whether sex is involved in the encounter on the threshing floor? If yes, why? If not, why not? How comfortable or uncomfortable does this type of question make you feel?

2 How might this chapter lead you in your imagination to an understanding of the lives of people who seem different from you?

3 How challenging is it for you to contemplate the possibility that someone from outside 'your group' could be capable of acting as the image of God towards you? What can you do to address this challenge?

Prayer

Strange God:

You speak from clouds and burning bushes,
from donkeys, death and devastating news.
You speak through stories of the past made relevant today.
You speak through mistakes we make
and through the things we do to keep ourselves alive.

If the far end of the horizon is no limit to you
then surely neither are we:
ourselves, our lovers, our enemies, those we troll,
those we denigrate, those we extol and lift to fame.

Whoever you are, speak to us, wherever we find ourselves.
And again, and again.
Plead with us, open us up with little stories,
small surprises that soften our guarded borders.

Because you are the strange voice
that speaks from strange places,
calling us – strangers all – towards each other
and towards a justice that looks like love.

Amen.

Discussion: Chapter 7

1 How could kindness find a place in the complex conversations and understandings that divide us?
2 If it is true that risk-taking kindness might draw similar
   from the other side of a political debate, what are the
   barriers to this kind of action and how can they be overcome?
3 In what ways might the complicated world of belonging
   invite us to make space for those we previously might
   have thought undeserving of that space?

Prayer

You gave us branches
that we carved into handles
for the swords we carried.

You gave us metals
that we mined and fashioned
into blades for the tops of spears.

You gave us land and we made
maps and drew borders on those maps,
building fences, making traps.

You gave us coal and sulphur
and we made bullets
out of things that could warm.

You took our sharp swords,
our handles for our weapons,
our bullets made for killing

and made them scythes and
ploughshares and hearths burning
brightly for hearts' imagining.

What we made sharp
you made sharper still,
imagining us into better being.

Discussion: Chapter 8

1 'So-and-So' imagines a future in which his half-Moabite
  children claim the land back from him, and in so doing he
  limits his interests today in order to protect himself from
  his fear-based fantasy of the future. Cuts off his nose to
  spite his face, we might say. Where have you seen this? In
  your own life? In the life of your community or country?

2 Can you think of situations in which the purity of a posi-
  tion on politics, borders or relationships was maintained
  despite obvious cost to all sides?

3 What is it that draws us to maintain our stance in the face
  of such cost? Think of examples from the recent history of
  your country, when acts of kindness had political impact;
  impact manifested in changed policy, action, provision
  and law.

Prayer

A confession:

There will be a time, we hear,
when our young will dream dreams
and our old will see visions.

Take those dreams and visions
– O God of night,
O God of day –
and shape them
in the shape of your creation.

We infuse our dreams with
visions of the other that
demeans the other
and depletes our love for one another.

Reveal us to ourselves.
Guide our dreams towards a resolution
that might lead us to imagine
others in your image,
not others in the image
of our worst nightmare.

Because your image
blooms with life and grows
and moves and breathes in
the night and the day.

Make this our dream,
make this our vision:
the flourishing of our hearts
in the presence of each other.

CPSIA information can be obtained
at www.ICGtesting.com
Printed in the USA
BVHW030604110123
655960BV00009B/66